# Current Chinese Economic Report Series



For further volumes:
http://www.springer.com/series/11028

Center for Macroeconomic Research
of Xiamen University

# China's Macroeconomic Outlook

## Quarterly Forecast and Analysis Report, August 2013

Springer

Center for Macroeconomic Research of Xiamen University
Center for Macroeconomic Research
Xiamen University
Xiamen, Fujian, China

ISSN 2194-7937 ISSN 2194-7945 (electronic)
ISBN 978-3-642-54220-6 ISBN 978-3-642-54221-3 (eBook)
DOI 10.1007/978-3-642-54221-3
Springer Heidelberg New York Dordrecht London

Library of Congress Control Number: 2014903495



Printed on acid-free paper

Springer is part of Springer Science+Business Media (www.springer.com)

# Preface

This report is a partial result of the "China Quarterly Macroeconomic Model (CQMM)", a project of the Center for Macroeconomic Research (CMR) in Xiamen University. The CMR is one of the Key Research Institutes of Humanities and Social Sciences of the Ministry of Education of China. The research is funded by the National Social Science Foundation of China (13&ZD029), the Key Research Institutes of Humanities and Social Sciences of the Ministry of Education of China (13JJD790025, 13JJD790026), and the Youth Project of National Social Science Foundation of China (13CJL017).

Since the launch of CQMM 7 years ago, 14 forecast reports with policy simulations and 7 essay collection books on China's macroeconomic analysis have been published. This is the 15th forecast report, which is a summary of forecast results released at the "China Macroeconomic Advanced Forum (Fall, 2013), CQMM Press Conference for Economic Projections for 2013–2014". The forum was jointly organized by the Center for Macroeconomic Research, Xiamen University, and the Economic Information Daily, Xinhua News Agency, in Beijing on August 18, 2013. Since the Fall of 2012, Springer began to publish the English version of these forecast and analysis report series entitled *China's Macroeconomic Outlook* twice a year.

We are grateful to all the participants for their valuable comments at the press conference. We revised the report based on their comments. We also appreciate support from Economic Information Daily, Xinhua News Agency. We thank the media for reporting the conference. Of course, we are fully responsible for all possible mistakes in this report.

Xiamen, Fujian
China

Center for Macroeconomic Research
of Xiamen University

# Preface

# Contents

# Contributors

**Principal Investigator**

**Wenpu Li** Center for Macroeconomic Research of Xiamen University, Xiamen, China

**Team Members**

Wang Yanwu, Gong Min, Liu Yu, Yu Changlin, Li Jing, Chen Guifu, Lin Zhiyuan, Lu Shengrong, Cui Qingwei, Xiong Ying, Wu Huakun, Huang Yanping, Luo Wei, Cao Cuirong, Li Hao, Xu Xinxin, Chen Tingting, Gao Hongjian

# Chapter 1
# Introduction

The sluggish external market demand and continuous domestic investment expansion in past years have caused excess production capacity, resulting in declines in the growth rate of value added of industry and GDP over the last 3 years in China. The slowdown of China's real economy in the first half of 2013 led to a significant decrease in the growth of government revenue, which in turn depressed the growth of government expenditure, especially the spending on people's wellbeing. Although the price level remained stable, the real income of urban and rural residents grew slowly, restraining final consumption from expanding. The main reason caused the imbalance of economic structure is the excess domestic investment, and the slowdown of the economy. In the first half of 2013, fixed asset investment was still primary driving force of China's economic growth. The excess domestic investment resulted mainly from the substantial increase of investment by state-owned or by state-holding enterprises, transportation or real estate industries, or from domestic loan.

For the second half of 2013, from the perspective of international economic environment, the euro-zone economy is expected to be still in recession, which will restrain China's export to Europe in; however, the United States as well as the developing countries is expected to experience a stable growth, which will promote China's exports. Based on IMF forecasts for the euro-zone and the United States for 2013–2014, our research team use the China Quarterly Macroeconomic Model (CQMM) to project China's macroeconomic outlook for the next six quarters. Our forecasts show that: the slowdown of economic growth will continue through 2013, and GDP growth rate will fall to 7.54 %, a decrease of 0.26 percentage points compared with the previous year; CPI is expected to stay at 2.45 %. The government revenue will continue to grow slowly at the level of 6.99 % in 2013, a decrease of 6.09 percentage points compared with the previous year; it will return to barely 7.87 % in 2014. Examined quarterly, GDP growth rate will fall to 7.46 % and 7.42 % in last two quarters of 2013, respectively.

Center for Macroeconomic Research of Xiamen University, *China's Macroeconomic Outlook*, Current Chinese Economic Report Series, DOI 10.1007/978-3-642-54221-3_1,

Although China is expected to achieve a growth rate of 7.5 % in 2013,[1] and to maintain price level stable, the slowdown of real economy, government revenue and real income of residents together with sluggish private investment demand will make the imbalance in economic structure more serious.

Due to a decline of the growth rate of public government revenue, the growth rate of government expenditure in people's wellbeing began to decrease faster than that of growth rate of spending on general public service, which will restrain spending on areas closely related to people's wellbeing and will be disadvantageous for China to transform economic growth pattern, to adjust economic structure and to increase resident incomes in line with economic growth.

The ratio of government revenue to GDP is one of the key ratios when dealing with the relationship between government power and market activities. How to collect government revenue[2] and how to spend it will have a great impact on the market economy order and on the realization of social development objective of China. Without regulation of government administration, market economy order will have no basis; without an honest, clean, low-cost and efficient government, a robust and efficient market economy would be a goal unreachable. To develop socialist market economy further, it's necessary to control the share of government revenue in national income, to restrict the power of central government and local governments, and to strengthen supervision and inspection of government administration and government budget. Because of slow growth of economy in the first half of 2013, the growth rate of public government revenue is lower than the growth rate of GDP. As government revenue grows slowly, the gap between government revenue and government spending become wider. Although Ministry of Finance and State Administration of Taxation have required to prohibit "excessive taxes",[3] some local governments still collect too much taxes, including "excessive taxes", "trivial taxes", and illegal fines, as a part of counter-cyclical policy.

Actually, to increase the tax revenue of central government, the share of local governments in total tax revenue had been dramatically reduced after a revenue-sharing reform in 1994,[4] while the duties of local governments as well as their

[1] The economic development target set by the that central government at the beginning of year 2013.

[2] Government Revenue refers to income for the government finance through participating in the distribution of social products. It is the financial guarantee to ensure government functioning. The government revenue includes the following main items: (1) Various tax revenues including domestic value added tax (VAT), domestic consumption tax, VAT and consumption tax from imports, VAT and consumption tax rebate for exports, business tax, corporate income tax, individual income tax, resource tax, city maintenance and construction tax, house property tax, stamp tax, urban land use tax, land appreciation tax, tax on vehicles and boat operation, ship tonnage tax, vehicle purchase tax, tariffs, farm land occupation tax, deed tax, and tobacco tax, etc. (2) Non-tax revenue, including special program receipts, charge of administrative and institutional units, penalty receipts and others non-tax receipts. http://www.stats.gov.cn/tjsj/ndsj/2012/html/zbe08.htm

[3] Refers to the practice of local governments that collect taxes for years to come in advance or more than legally allowed.

[4] Which decreased the proportion of local governments revenue in total government tax revenue from 78 to 44 % in that single year.

spending have not been reduced accordingly. Therefore, local governments are forced to collect revenue through non-tax channels. The proportion of non-tax revenue in public government revenue has been rising from 5.4 % in 1994 to 14.2 % in 2012. In China, local governments greatly rely on non-tax revenue: 80 % of non-tax revenue in China is collected by local governments, while only 20 % by central government. Non-tax revenue accounts for 20 % of fiscal revenue of local governments, while it accounts for only 5 % of fiscal revenue of central government.

When collecting government revenue, it is essential to guard against subjectivism and arbitrariness. Therefore, non-tax revenue should be minimized because it is too arbitrary, and it lacks normalization, openness, fairness. Firstly, increasing the proportion of non-tax revenue will increase the burden of residents and enterprises, especially small and medium-sized enterprises. Secondly, since the local governments' actions are too arbitrary and there's no definite rule to follow, the residents and enterprises can't make good expectations about the future, which leads to higher transaction cost in the process of economic operation, and the unnecessary transaction cost will reduce efficiency and productivity, restrain residents' consumption expanding, and affect economic growth. Thirdly, the present tax system facilitates illegal activities and leave too many loopholes for corruption. To establish and develop socialist market economy, it's essential to handle the relationship between government power and market activities, to control the scale of government revenue and spending, and to standardize government administration. For the reasons above, our research team pays special attention to the effect on economic growth and structural adjustment of controlling government revenue, decreasing the proportion of non-tax revenue and alleviating burden of enterprises and residents.

So our research team supposes that: if the share of non-tax revenue in government revenue had dropped to 10 % during 2007–2012, then the government non-tax revenue would have decreased by 63.07, 108.17, 238.32, 175.62, 416.51 and 545.99 billion Yuan each year respectively. At the same time, the reduced revenue could be transferred to enterprises or workers.

The simulation result shows that the effects of reducing non-tax revenue of local governments in government revenue are quite optimistic: the government tax revenue will increase because the decrease of non-tax revenue could be compensated by increase of tax-revenue due to growth of economy; the ratio of government revenue to GDP would not fall significantly. The reduced non-tax revenue were redistributed to enterprises and residents, and this redistribution would alleviate the tax burden of enterprises and residents and play a positive role in promoting economic growth, reducing the excess production capacity, adjusting economic structure, expanding consumer demand, stimulating real economy investment, increasing taxes and so forth.

Exceptionally high ratio of government revenue to GDP has a negative effect on economic growth, economic structure adjustment and expansion of consumption. Therefore, to regulate government behaviors in collecting revenue by reducing non-tax revenue will lower the ratio of government revenue to GDP to a certain degree. In addition, regulating government behaviors in collecting revenue is advantageous to promote administration in accordance with the laws, rules and regulations, enhance the transparency and fairness of government management, promote formulation of normal market economy order, and help formulate consistent expectation of participants (enterprises and residents) in the market towards government administration.

On the basis of forecasts and simulation results, our research team puts forward the following policy recommendations.

1. Although economic growth is slowing down, China still has a good chance to achieve the economic development target which is to increase GDP by 7.5 % and to keep price level stable. While macroeconomic policy authority should always keep an eye on economic trends at home and abroad, take precautions to carry out timely and appropriate anticipatory adjustments and fine-tuning to ensure the realization of economic growth target.
2. The reason that the growth rate of government revenue will fall in 2013 mainly lies in economic slowdown and economic system adjustment, but it still is higher than 7.5 % because that structure of government revenue has not substantially changed. Moreover, this is an opportunity to reform the revenue system. It should begin with transformation of the pattern of economic development and adjustment of economic structure, then take advantage of the opportunity to reduce the fiscal expenditures and adjust structure of fiscal expenditures.
3. It is impossible that government revenue grows faster than the economy for a long period, and overhigh proportion of the government revenue will seriously impede the development of market economy. Therefore, it's essential to control the growth rate and proportion of government revenue in GDP, to standardize sources of revenue and government administration in collecting revenue through economic system adjustment. On the other hand, it is also essential to reduce the share of non-tax revenue in public government revenue gradually, to adjust structure of fiscal expenditures, to ensure that expenditures on people's wellbeing grow steadily and to reduce cost of general public service.
4. To improve socialist market economy, fiscal revenue should not grow faster the GDP in long-term. So government must be low-cost in the long run as well as in the short run, it should be carried out to streamline government departments at all levels and establish small government. In addition, strengthening administrative and budgetary oversight by the public are needed.
5. Reducing non-tax revenue and standardizing government administration of collecting revenue can lower the proportion of government revenue. It's helpful to reduce government revenue and thus reduce the proportion of government revenue in GDP, and at the same time it is advantageous to promote administration in accordance with laws, rules and regulations, enhance the transparency and fairness of government management, promote formulation of normal market economy order, and help participants in the market to formulate consistent expectation towards government administration. Most of non-tax revenue is collected by local governments, and this phenomenon exists mainly because of the unreasonable fiscal system, especially the revenue system. We should reform fiscal system and adjust the economic rights and duties between central government and local governments, and strive to match the rights and duties. Both central and local initiative should be brought into play with clear responsibility of each party.

6. Special attention should be paid to areas closely related to the people's wellbeing such as education, scientific technology, culture and recreation, medical and health care, social security and employment, and the government should prevent expenditure from declining sharply in these areas. To reduce government overhead, we should strictly control the construction and expansion of government office buildings, and plug up loopholes in management rules by banning the construction of more luxury government building and halls with excuses of people's wellbeing program or using some fabricated titles such as "civil service center ". We suggest that government should adjust statistical classification of public expenditure, distinguish administrative expenditure and service expenditure on people's wellbeing clearly, and this suggestion is advantageous to auditing and oversight from higher authorities and the public, and is also helpful to reduce the administrative cost and establish a service-oriented government.

China's economic development since the global financial crisis (specially from this year) has shown some new characteristics as follows: facing with uncertainties abroad and at home, China's development potential under current economic system is experiencing a downward pressure and the investment-driven pattern of economic growth is not sustainable. The efficiency of investment drops down, thus the tie between investment and economic growth becomes not as tight as before. Apparently, if we don't further deepen all-round reform in social economic system, develop and improve socialist market economy, release economic development potential and start a new engine for economic development as soon as possible, the decline of economic growth due to economic structural imbalance will continue. Our research team suggests that stabilizing potential growth rate is possible essentially by further deepening reform in social economic reform, expanding effective supply, enhancing efficiency of investment, and thus raising labor productivity. Therefore, we must trigger a new round of reform in social and economic system, develop and improve socialist market economy further, promote to compete on an equal basis, explore the space of resource optimization, correct the distortion of relative prices of factors, adjust economic structure, improve government public administration, lighten the burden on enterprises, enhance efficiency of supply, release economic development potential and foster domestic demand. The new round overall reform in social economic system will not only expand China's economic development space tremendously, maintain steady growth of China's economy, but also become an institutional guarantee for transferring the pattern of economic development, transition from a middle-income economy to a higher stage.

# Chapter 2
# A Review of China's Economy in the First Half of 2013

In the first half of 2013, China's industrial production grew slowly, economic growth rate continued to decline, and the growth rate of government revenue fell sharply because of the sluggish external market demand as well as domestic excess production capacity; the expansion of consumption demand could not continue due to the slowdown in the growth rate of real income of urban and rural residents; therefore, the investment in fixed assets was still the main driving force of economic growth. Looking forward to the second half of 2013, the euro-zone economy continued to shrink, and Chinese exports to Europe will be restrained; on the other hand, the steady economic growth of the USA and the developing countries will be conducive to China's exports. However, the slow growth of domestic real economy, government revenue, resident real income and private investment demand have become the important obstacles to growth of China's economy. Overall, China's economic growth in 2013 may achieve 7.5 %, the target set by the central government, and the price level may be stable. To achieve China's economic targets and to ensure that China's economy will maintain the growth rate within a reasonable range, the macroeconomic policy authority of China should still take precautions according to the dynamic of the economic development, carry out timely and appropriate anticipatory adjustments and fine-tuning, and make policies more targeted, flexible, and anticipatory. Meanwhile, to ensure that China's economy will grow sustainably, China needs to launch a new round of reform of social and economic systems, to develop and improve the socialist market economy, to promote equal competition, to optimize resource allocation, to correct price distortions, to adjust the economic structure, to improve the government's public management, to reduce the burden of enterprises, to improve supply efficiency, to release the economic growth potential, to foster domestic demand. All these works will in favor of the social and economic development and transformation, the smooth transition from the middle-income economies to a higher stage of development.

Center for Macroeconomic Research of Xiamen University, *China's Macroeconomic Outlook*, Current Chinese Economic Report Series, DOI 10.1007/978-3-642-54221-3_2,

## 2.1 Economic Growth Slowed Down, Structural Imbalance Persisted

The growth rate of China's industrial production and gross domestic product (GDP) continued to decline (Fig. 2.1) because of the weak external market demand and domestic excess production capacity. The growth rate of cumulative industrial added value fell from 19.6 % in the first quarter of 2010 to 9.3 % in the second quarter of 2013, and GDP growth rate also fell from 12.1 to 7.6 %, both reached their nadirs within nearly 3 years.

Based on the expenditure accounting approach, the cumulative contribution rate of investment to GDP growth increased from 30.3 % in the first quarter to 53.9 % in the first half year of 2013 meanwhile, the cumulative contribution rate of final consumption to GDP growth decreased from 55.5 % to 45.2 %, an decrease of 5.2 percentage points over the previous year; the cumulative contribution rate of net outflow of goods and services to GDP was 0.9 %. Therefore, China's economy continued to slow down, meanwhile, the structural imbalance persisted; investment was still the main driving force of economic growth in the first half of 2013.

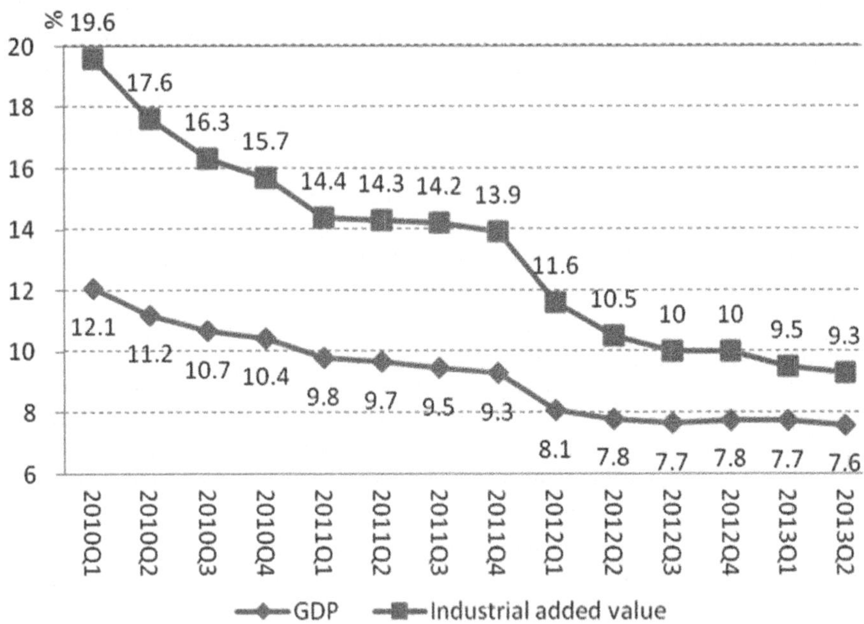


**Fig. 2.1** The changes in the growth rate of GDP and industrial added value (on year-on-year basis) from 2010 to 2013 (Data Source: CEIC Data)

## 2.2 Manufacturing Investment Growth Fell Sharply, Transportation Investment Grew Fast

In the first half of 2013, urban cumulative fixed asset investment increased by 20.1 %, a decrease of 0.3 percentage points over the previous year. In terms of industries, the cumulative growth rate of investment in the manufacturing sectors was 17.1 %, a decrease of 7.4 percentage points over the previous year, the lowest growth rate within a decade; the cumulative growth rate of investment in real estate was 22.9 %, an increase of 0.8 percentage points over the previous year; the cumulative growth rate of investment in transportation, storage and postal services was 21.5 %, an increase of 23.5 percentage points over the previous year (Fig. 2.2). A sharp drop in the cumulative growth rate of manufacturing investment has reflected the slowdown in the real economy, as well as excess production capacity in the first half of 2013.

In the first half of 2013, in terms of the sources of budgets, the growth rate of investment from the central budget was 9.7 %, an increase of 13.8 percentage points over the previous year; the growth rate of investment from budget of the local governments was 20.7 %, a decrease of 1.4 percentage points over the previous year.

In terms of the types of investors, the cumulative growth rate of investment from state-owned and state holding enterprises was 17.5 %, an increase of 3.7 percentage points over the previous year; the cumulative growth rate of investment from Hong

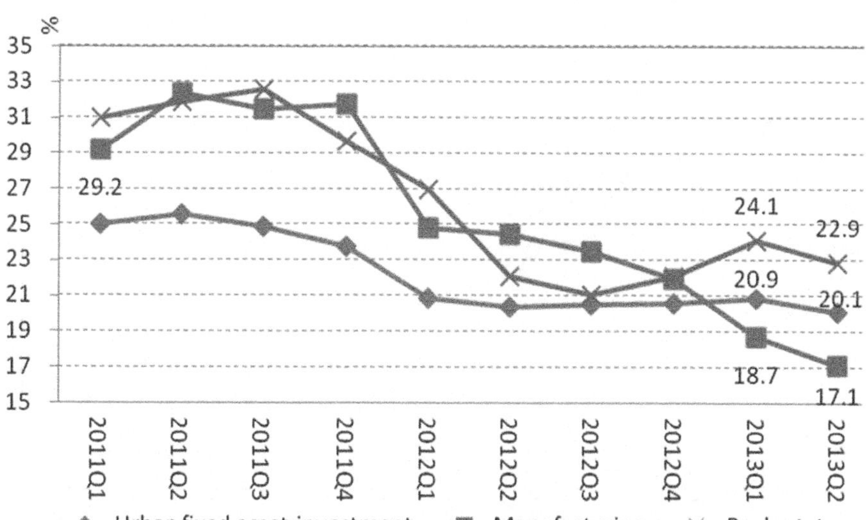


**Fig. 2.2** On year-on-year basis, the cumulative growth rate of urban fixed asset investment and its industry component (Data Source: CEIC Data)

Kong, Macao and Taiwan's enterprises was 7.5 %, a decrease of 3.7 percentage points over the previous year; the cumulative growth rate of investment from foreign enterprises was 3.9 %, a decrease of 10 percentage points over the previous year. In terms of finance sources, the growth rate of investment from domestic loans was 13 %, an increase of 7.2 percentage points over the previous year; the growth rate of investment from self-raised fund was 18.6 %, a decrease of 4.3 percentage points over the previous year; the growth rate of foreign investment was –8.4 %, a decrease of 2.9 percentage points over the previous year. It can be said that the external market demand shocks and domestic excess production capacity have led to a significant decline in the growth rate of investment in non-state-owned enterprises in the first half of 2013; A substantial increase in the growth rate of investment by state-owned and state holding enterprises, domestic loans and transportation (and real estate) sector is an important factor in the steady growth of fixed asset investment in the first half of 2013.

## 2.3 The Growth of Imports and Exports Was Weak, the Trade Surplus Continued to Expand

In the first half of 2013, the weak demand from major countries, the continued appreciation of the RMB and the increase in wages have led to the weak growth of China's imports and exports. The total exports in dollars increased by 10.4 %, only up 1.3 percentage points over the previous year; the total imports grew by 6.7 %, the same as the previous year (Fig. 2.3). The cumulative trade surplus reached 107.95

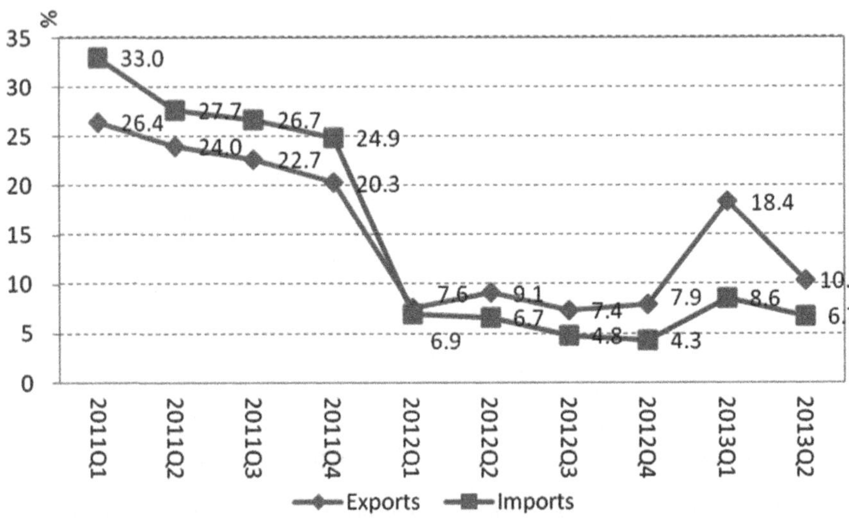


**Fig. 2.3** The cumulative year-on-year growth of nominal export and import (Data Source: CEIC Data)

billion dollars, an increase of 57.4 % over the previous year. Total utilized foreign direct investment increased by 4.8 %, an increase of 7.8 percentage points over the previous year; new foreign exchange reserves stood at 185.1 billion dollars.

In terms of trade composition, in the first half of 2013, general trade exports increased by 10 %, a drop of 0.1 percentage points over the previous year; general trade imports increased by 3 %, a drop of 4.8 percentage points over the previous year; trade deficit of general trade cumulatively totaled 23.3 billion dollars. The growth rate of processing trade exports declined 0.9 %, a decrease of 7.3 percentage points over the previous year; and that of imports in processing trade grew by 4.6 %, an increase of 3.9 percentage points over the previous year; trade surplus of processing trade reduced to 172.9 billion dollars.

In terms of imports and exports by regions, in the first half of 2013, the growth rate of China's exports dropped by 2.1 % to Europe, by 1.7 % to the U.S., and by 20.1 % to Asia. The share of China's exports to Europe in total exports was 17.8 % in the first half of 2013, a decrease of 2.3 percentage points over the previous year; the share of exports to the U.S. was 16.0 %, a decrease of 1.3 percentage points; the share of China's exports to Asia was 52.7 %, an increase of 4.3 percentage points over the previous year.

From the import side, in the first half of 2013, the growth rate of China's imports increased by 7.3 % from Europe, by 15.1 % from the U.S., and by 7.3 % from Asia; the share of imports in three regions was roughly stable.

## 2.4 The Growth Rate of Real Income Declined, the Growth of Domestic Consumption Slowed Down

In the first half of 2013, the per capita disposable income of urban residents was only 13,649 Yuan, due to the slowdown of the wage income; the real growth rate was 6.5 %, lower than the growth rate of GDP in the same period; a decrease of 1.1 percentage points compared with the same period of 2011, a decrease of 3.2 percentage points compared with the same period of 2012. As the price of agricultural products declined, the per capita cash income of rural residents was 4817 Yuan in the first half of 2013, the real growth rate was 9.2 %; a decrease of 4.5 percentage points compared with the same period of 2011, a decrease of 3.2 percentage points compared with the same period of 2012 (Fig. 2.4). The growth rate of real income of urban and rural residents dropped sharply, and then consumption demand could not expand.

The total retail sales of consumption goods only increased by 12.7 % in the first half of 2013, a decrease of 1.7 percentage points over the previous year, the lowest growth rate since 2008. Among the total retail sales, urban area accounted for 85 %, and rural area for 15 %. Total retail sales in urban areas rose by 12.5 %, a decrease of 1.8 percentage points over the previous year; and it increased by 14.3 % in rural areas, a decrease of 0.2 percentage points. According to the household survey data,

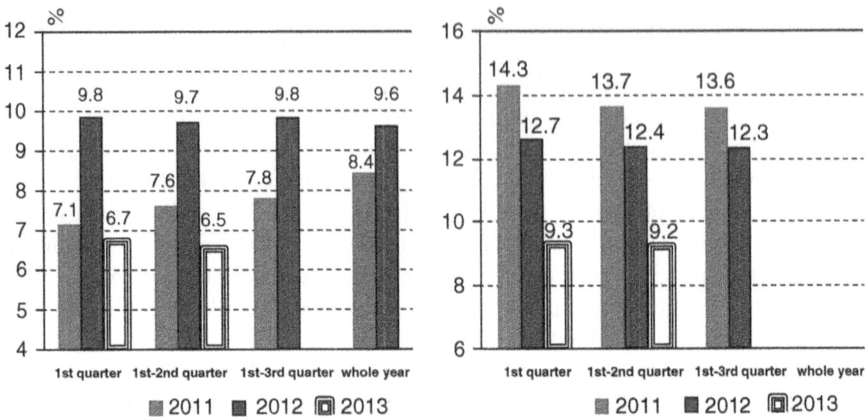


**Fig. 2.4** The cumulative year-on-year real growth rate of urban per capita disposable income and rural per capita cash income (Note: The National Bureau of Statistics does not publish the year-on-year real growth rate of the per capita cash income of rural residents at the end of the year. Data Source: CEIC Data)

the cumulative per capita consumption of urban residents grew by 7.2 % in the first half of 2013, a decrease of 4.2 percentage points compared with the same period in 2011, a decrease of 4.8 percentage points compared with the same period in 2012. The cumulative per capita cash expenditure of rural residents rose by 12.8 %, a decrease of 10.3 percentage points compared with the same period in 2011, a decrease of 3.8 percentage points compared with the same period in 2012.

## 2.5 CPI Changed Smoothly, PPI Continued to Fall

In June 2013 (Fig. 2.5), the consumer price index (CPI) rose by 2.7 % over the same period of previous year, of which 70.4 % was contributed by the carryover effect, 29.6 % by current price factors. The CPI excluding food and energy rose by 1.7 %, the non-food CPI rose by 1.6 %. The CPI changed mildly in the first half of 2013. On the other hand, the industrial producer price index (PPI) continued to decline.

In June 2013, the PPI fell to 2.7 %, and would fall further. Decline in PPI likely resulted from the decline in commodity prices[1]; and it reflected the excess production capacity of some industries, such as iron and steel, coal, glass, aluminum, photovoltaic, cement.

[1]The Dow Jones-UBS Commodity index showed that commodity prices decreased by about 46 % compared with the peak in 2008.

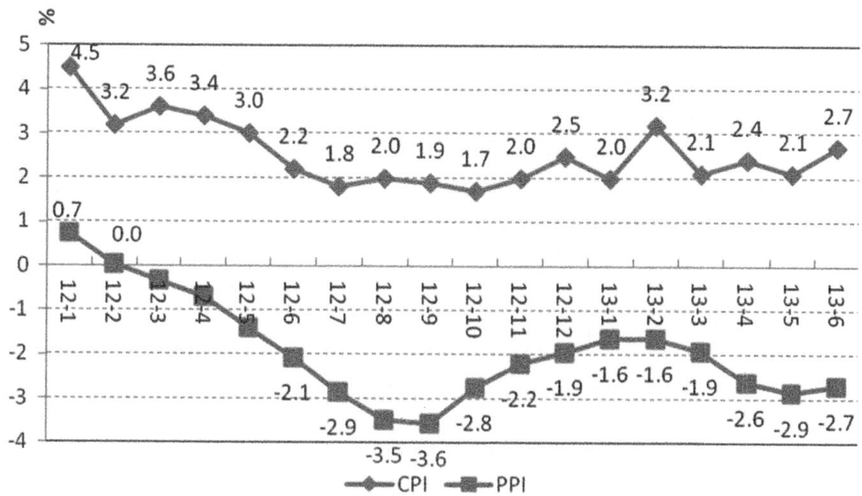


**Fig. 2.5** The monthly year-on-year growth rate of the consumer price index (CPI) and the industrial producer price index (PPI) (Data Source: CEIC Data)

## 2.6 The Monetary Policy Was Tightening Gradually and the Fiscal Policy Was Fine-Tuning Actively

The monetary policy basically maintained a steady tightening situation in the first half of 2013. Broad money supply (M2) grew by 15.7 % in the first quarter and 14 % in the second quarter, a decrease of 2.46 and 4.47 percentage points over the previous year respectively. At the end of June, currency in circulation (M0) increased by 9.7 %, a decrease of 1.1 percentage points over the previous year. The balance of RMB loans increased by 14.2 % in the first half of 2013, a decrease of 1.8 percentage points over the previous year; new loans reached 5.1 trillion Yuan, 221.8 billion Yuan more than the same period of last year. Among the new loans, the real estate accounted for about 25.6 %, an increase of nearly 14 percentage points over the previous year. At the same time, the "total amount of social financing" grew rapidly in the first half of 2013, the year-on-year growth rate reaching 30.5 % until June of 2013. New loans accounted for 50 % of total amount of social financing, a decrease of 19.9 percentage points over the previous year (Fig. 2.6).

In the first half of 2013, the manufacturing investment and economic growth decreased, while the monetary and credit expanded. This showed that the slowdown in real economy had directly inhibited the willingness to invest in the real economy, and then the effect of monetary policy was restrained. On the other hand, this showed that the most new loans had gone into the real estate industry, which

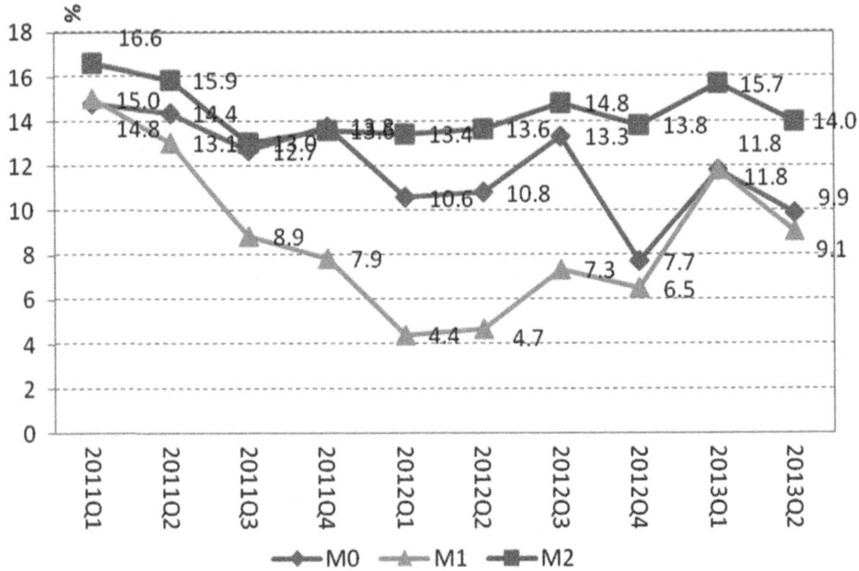


**Fig. 2.6** The year-on-year growth rate of the money supply (Data Source: CEIC Data)

restricted by new government's regulation, rather than into the real economy. The most important one is that the driving effects of investment on economic growth were weak under the current pattern of economic growth, and the financial system had less effect on the economic growth.

On fiscal policy, in the first half of 2013, government revenue increased by 7.5 %, a decrease of 4.7 percentage points over the previous year (Fig. 2.7). The tax revenue only grew by 7.9 % in the first half of 2013, a decrease of 1.9 percentage points over the previous year due to the slowdown in the industrial production; government non-tax revenue increased by 5.3 %, a decrease of 24.2 percentage points over the previous year. In terms of the composition of government revenue, tax revenue accounted for 86.4 %, an increase of 0.3 percentage points over the previous year; non-tax revenue accounted for 13.6 %.

In tax revenue, the cumulative growth rate of corporate income tax was 14.2 %, a decrease of 3.1 percentage points over the previous year, accounting for 25.3 % of the total tax revenue; the cumulative growth rate of the value added tax was 6.6 %, a decrease of 1.45 percentage points, accounting for 24.2 % of the total tax revenue; the cumulative growth rate of the sales tax was 12.9 %, an increase of 3.2 percentage points over the previous year, accounting for 14.9 % of the total tax revenue. In addition, the decline in the growth rate of the general trade imports also led to the negative growth of the consumption tax and value added tax of the imported goods.

The growth rate of government expenditure decreased greatly due to the decline in the growth of government revenue (Fig. 2.7). The cumulative growth rate of government expenditure was 10.8 % until June, a decrease of 10.5 percentage points over the previous year, the lowest growth rate in recent years.

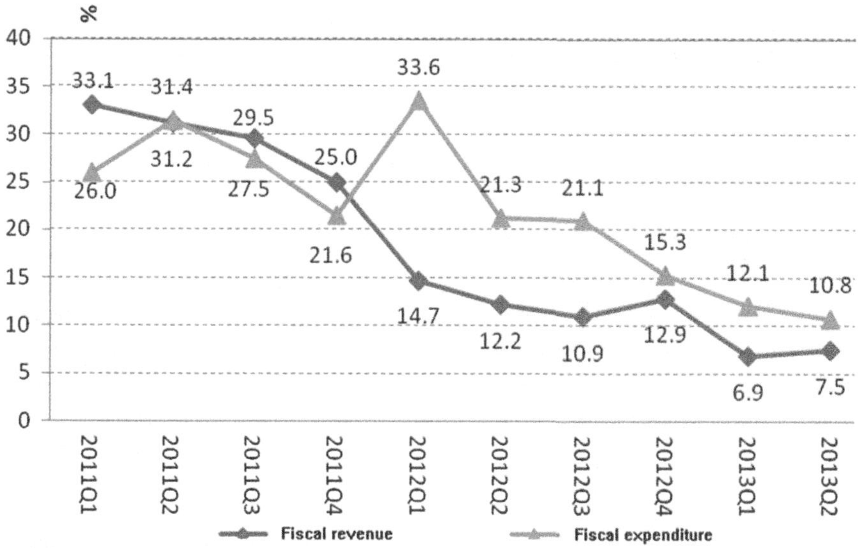


**Fig. 2.7** The year-on-year nominal growth of fiscal revenue and expenditure (Data Source: CEIC Data)

In terms of the composition of government expenditure, the cumulative growth of the general public service expenditure was 14.8 %, a decrease of 3.8 percentage points over the previous year, accounting for 10.4 % of the total government expenditure; the cumulative growth of expenditures related to people's wellbeing, such as education, science and technology, culture, sports and media, health care, social security and employment, was 14.8 %, a decrease of 6.2 percentage points (Fig. 2.8), accounting for 38.5 % of the total government expenditure. From the beginning of the year, the fiscal policy authority has introduced many fine-tuning measures[2] to improve government fiscal situation. However, reducing the growth rate of the expenditure in the areas related to people's wellbeing due to budget constraint is obviously not conductive to promoting the adjustment of economic structure, as well as the transformation of pattern of economic development, under the fact that the real economy is slowing down, and the relationship between investment and economic growth is increasingly weak.

In conclusion, in the first half of 2013, industrial production grew slowly, economic growth rate continued to decline, and the growth rate of government revenue fell sharply due to the weak external market demand as well as domestic excess production capacity. Although the price level remained stable, the expansion of

[2]As introduced in July to reduce the government general public service expenditure 5 %, some fine-tuning measures have been implemented across the country since August 1, such as "replacing the business tax with a value-added tax", stopping the construction of luxurious government office buildings and halls, tax relief for small businesses, optimizing administrative measures for export enterprises and safeguarding railway capital construction and so forth.

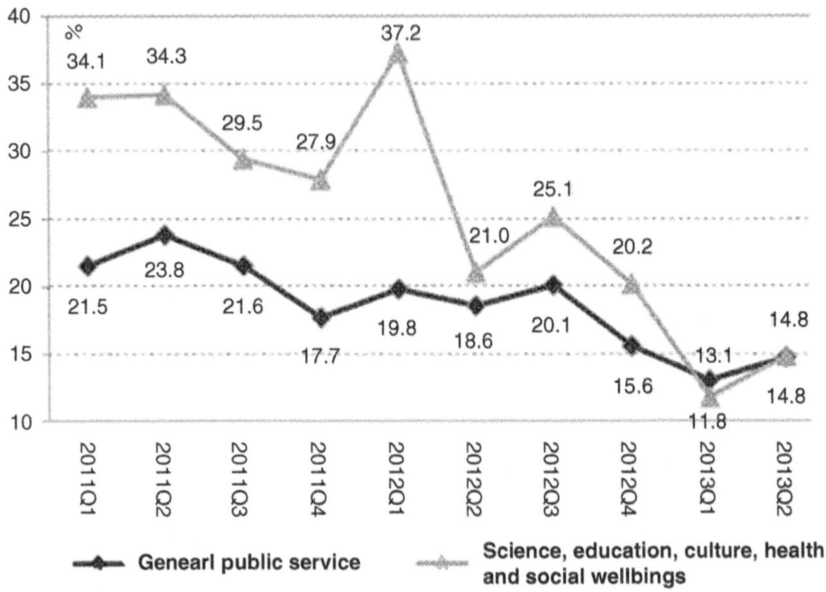


**Fig. 2.8** The year-on-year growth rate of government expenditure of people's livelihood in a narrow sense (Data Source: CEIC Data)

consumption demand was inhibited due to the slowdown in the growth rate of real income of urban and rural residents. A substantial increase in the growth rate of investment by state-owned enterprises, domestic loans and transportation industry, to some extent, offset the decline in the growth rate of investment in the private manufacturing sector; therefore, the growth of investment in fixed asset could keep steady. Investment was still the main driving force of economic growth, and the problem of economic structural imbalance remained unsolved. In the second half of 2013, although the recovery of the world economy will help to ease the pressure on a continuing fall in the growth of China's exports, the Chinese economy in 2013 is expected to achieve 7.5 %, a target set by the central government. However, the economic structural imbalance would worsen. Especially, under the background of the decline in the growth of government revenue, the growth rate of expenditure for people's wellbeing in the fiscal expenditure will decline more sharply than the growth rate of expenditure in the general public services of government, and the growth rate of real income of urban and rural residents will decrease. The above negative effects will hinder transformation of pattern of economic development, the adjustment of the economic structural imbalance, and the effort to increase real per capita income of residents to be in step with economic growth of the country.

# Chapter 3
# Forecast of China's Economy During 2013–2014

## 3.1 Improvements of CQMM

Since the launch of CQMM in 2006, the model have been geared to the changes and development of China's economy; improvements of CQMM have been made in succession to capture the characters of China's economic development more accurately, to improve the precision of forecast and to enhance the effect of policy simulation.

Two modifications have been made to extend the model in this version Firstly, aggregate supply module is introduced, making CQMM from a model based on demand side to a balanced aggregate structural model, which provides a more powerful tool for analysis from the perspective of interaction of aggregate demand and aggregate supply. Taking advantage of this improvement, the excess production capacity in China has been measured and policies which have effects on the adjustments of excess production capacity have been discussed. Secondly, the finance module has been further improved. Government revenues and expenditures has been endogenized, thereby discussions of the interactions between economic growth and public finance become feasible.

### *3.1.1 Introducing Production Function and Measuring the Output Gap*

The aggregate production function was estimated after quarterly time series of capital and employment was calculated. Thus, the variables of supply side, such as wage and industrial profit, become endogenous. On this basis, the potential output and the output gap can be computed. As a result, CQMM can not only catch the mechanism of China's economy more precisely, but also expand its application to new fields.

Using the Hodrick-Prescott filter to compute the output gap is a usual method. However, the output gap computed by HP filter is a theoretic value and it is different from the true value. As shown in Fig. 3.1, the HP filter method indicates no excess

Center for Macroeconomic Research of Xiamen University, *China's Macroeconomic Outlook*, Current Chinese Economic Report Series, DOI 10.1007/978-3-642-54221-3_3,

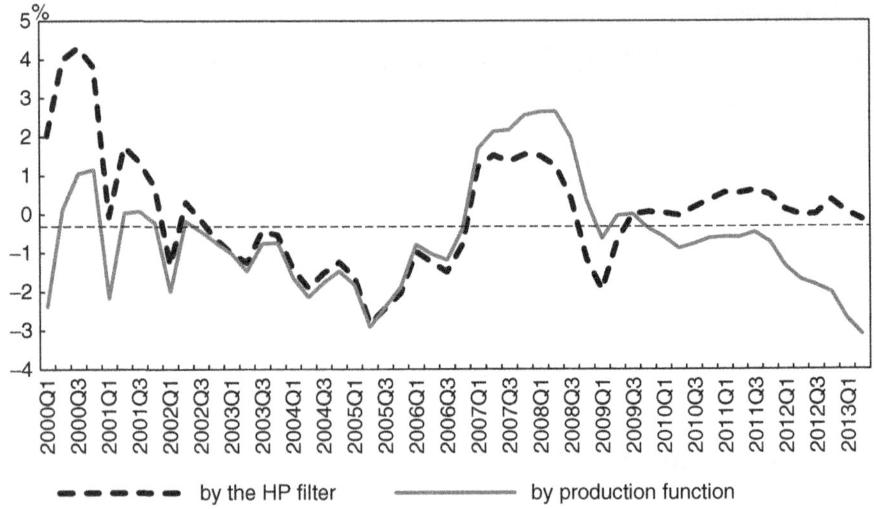


**Fig. 3.1** Output gap computed by CQMM

production capacity in recent years, which is against economic intuition. In contrast, CQMM suggest that the output gap have been continually increasing since 2009, which is in accordance with the actual observation. It shows that the expansionary fiscal and monetary policies which respond to global financial crisis in past 3 or 4 years have caused excess production capacity, not only in terms of economic aggregates but also in terms of industrial structure.

### *3.1.2 Improvement of the Fiscal Module*

To improve the previous model, government revenue has been introduced as an endogenous variable, making it possible to investigate the effect of economic slowdown on government revenue. Assuming non-tax revenue to be an exogenous variable, the equations of government revenue have been set up to depict the relations between economic growth and the public finance or its structure.

## 3.2 Assumptions of Exogenous Variables

### *3.2.1 Economic Growth Rates in the Euro Zone and the U.S.*

In the first half of 2013, the euro area remained in recession, with a contraction of 1.1 % (annual rate after season adjustment) in the first quarter of 2013. It is reasonable to assume that the economy of the euro- area keeps declining. The updated

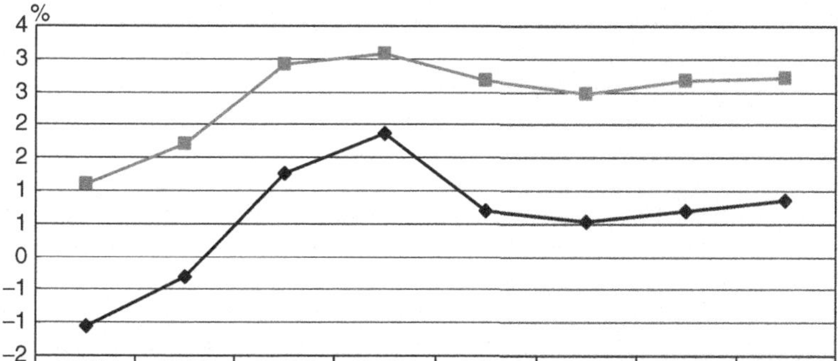


| | 2013Q1 | 2013Q2 | 2013Q3 | 2013Q4 | 2014Q1 | 2014Q2 | 2014Q3 | 2014Q4 |
|---|---|---|---|---|---|---|---|---|
| EU17GDP_C | −1.06 | −0.31 | 1.26 | 1.86 | 0.69 | 0.53 | 0.69 | 0.85 |
| USGDP_C | 1.10 | 1.70 | 2.92 | 3.09 | 2.68 | 2.47 | 2.68 | 2.72 |

**Fig. 3.2** Assumptions of growth in the United States and the Euro area (Note: EU17GDP_C denotes growth in the euro area, while USGDP_C denotes growth in the US)

outlook from IMF in July, 2013, suggests that growth in the euro area in 2013 would be −0.6 %, further lower than the previous estimation published in January. On the other hand, as the slowly decreasing unemployment rate and growing private residential spending, the U.S. economy expanded at a steady pace. For annual rate after season adjustment, growth in the United States increased from 1.1 % in the first quarter to 1.7 % in the second quarter of 2013. However, IMF projected that growth in the United States would average at 1.7 % in 2013, and rise to 2.7 % in 2014, while growth in the euro area would turn to 0.9 % in 2014. Taking account of these information, growth in these two areas are projected to rebound in the second half of 2013 and to keep steady in 2014 (Fig. 3.2).

### 3.2.2 *Major Exchange Rates*

The euro is expected to be further weakening against the US dollar in the second half of 2013, with regard to both the slowdown of the economy of the euro area and the recovery of the economy of the United States. The exchange rate of the euro against the US dollar will fall to 1:1.27 in the last quarter of 2013, and then return to 1:1.28 in 2014, with support from gradually stabilizing economy. Meanwhile, the RMB is forecast to have a trend of long-term appreciation as well as a short-term fluctuation. Dragged down by the uncertainties of global economy, China's export growth will slow down, resulting in less trade surplus and capital inflows. All these factors will ease the appreciation pressure on the RMB and make the appreciation of RMB not as fast as before. The exchange rate of the RMB against the US dollar is projected to be 1:6.11 at the end of 2013, and 1:6.03 at the end of 2014 (Fig. 3.3).

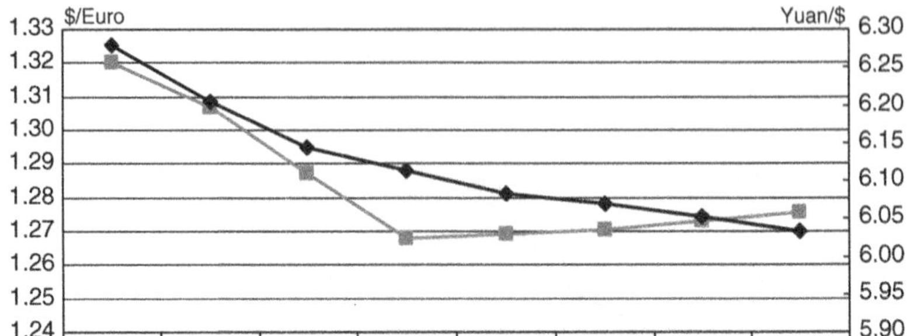


| | 2013Q1 | 2013Q2 | 2013Q3 | 2013Q4 | 2014Q1 | 2014Q2 | 2014Q3 | 2014Q4 |
|---|---|---|---|---|---|---|---|---|
| USDEURO | 1.32 | 1.31 | 1.29 | 1.27 | 1.27 | 1.27 | 1.27 | 1.28 |
| ER_W | 6.28 | 6.21 | 6.14 | 6.11 | 6.08 | 6.07 | 6.05 | 6.03 |

**Fig. 3.3** Assumptions of major exchange rates (Note: ER_W denotes the exchange rate of the RMB against the US dollar, and USDEURO denotes the exchange rate of the US dollar against the euro)

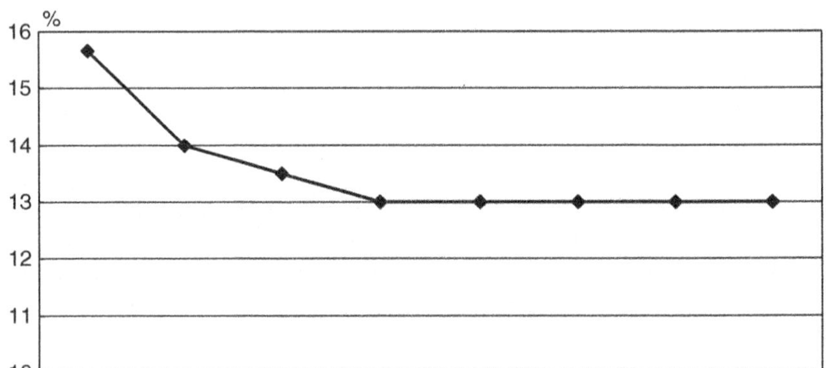


| | 2013Q1 | 2013Q2 | 2013Q3 | 2013Q4 | 2014Q1 | 2014Q2 | 2014Q3 | 2014Q4 |
|---|---|---|---|---|---|---|---|---|
| M2 | 15.7 | 14.0 | 13.5 | 13 | 13 | 13 | 13 | 13 |

**Fig. 3.4** Assumption of the growth rate of M2

### 3.2.3 *The Growth Rate of Broad Money Supply (M2)*

The sluggish domestic real economy in the first half of 2013 weakened the willingness to invest in real industries such as manufacturing, and the proportion of newly increased loan using for real estate investment rose rapidly. Our model assumes that the monetary policy will follow the principle of "restrict growth and revitalize stock", and tighten up with a gradual and steady pace, to avoid the increase in asset price. Compared with the same quarter of previous year, the growth rate of M2 is expected to fall to 13.5 % in the third quarter of 2013, and to keep a growth of 13 % for all the rest periods (Fig. 3.4). Furthermore, the benchmark lending rate is expected to remain at current level of 6 %.

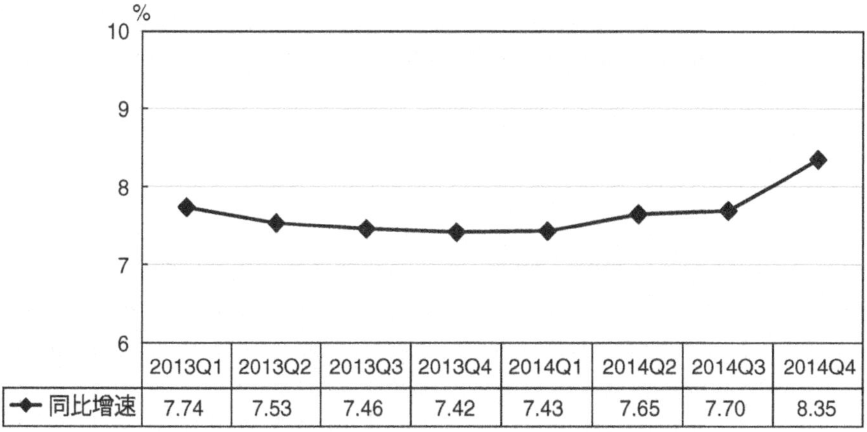


**Fig. 3.5** Forecast of GDP growth rate (on year-on-year basis)

## 3.3 Forecasts of China's Major Macroeconomic Indicators for 2013–2014

### *3.3.1 Forecast of GDP Growth*

Given assumptions of exogenous variables, growth in China is expected to evolve at a more moderate pace in the second half of 2013, 7.46 % in the third quarter and 7.42 % in the fourth quarter, averaging 7.54 in whole year, which is 0.26 percentage points less than that in 2012. However, it is expected to return to 7.79 % in 2014. All these results are shown below (Fig. 3.5).[1]

### *3.3.2 Forecasts of Major Price Indices*

Inflation in China is anticipated to be stable in 2013, as a result of weaker growth and stable prices of major commodities on the world market. CPI will fall to 2.45 % in 2013, 0.19 percentage points less than in the previous year, and further fall to 1.79 % in 2014. In the second half of 2013, CPI will reach the peak of 2.58 % in the third quarter and then fall to 2.37 % respectively in the fourth quarter over the previous year (Fig. 3.6).

PPI will keep negative, and be −1.71 % in 2013 and −0.97 % in 2014, respectively. In particular, the PPI will be −1.15 and −0.78 % in last quarters of 2013 and 2014 over the previous year, respectively, as shown in Fig. 3.6.

[1] Forecast values in this report are all after season adjustment.

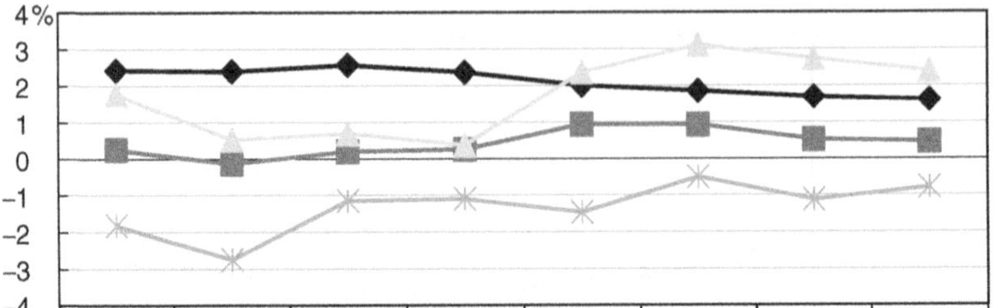


| | 2013Q1 | 2013Q2 | 2013Q3 | 2013Q4 | 2014Q1 | 2014Q2 | 2014Q3 | 2014Q4 |
|---|---|---|---|---|---|---|---|---|
| CPI | 2.43 | 2.41 | 2.58 | 2.37 | 2.01 | 1.86 | 1.69 | 1.61 |
| P_I | 0.25 | −0.13 | 0.20 | 0.26 | 0.93 | 0.92 | 0.52 | 0.46 |
| P_GDP | 1.78 | 0.52 | 0.69 | 0.37 | 2.37 | 3.11 | 2.74 | 2.40 |
| PPI | −1.82 | −2.75 | −1.15 | −1.10 | −1.46 | −0.50 | −1.12 | −0.78 |

**Fig. 3.6** Forecasts of major price indices (on year-on-year basis) (Note: CPI, P_I, P_GDP and PPI denote consumer price index, price index of investment in fixed assets, GDP deflator and producer price index, respectively)

The price index of investment in fixed assets (P_I) is anticipated to be 0.14 % in 2013, a decrease of 0.96 percentage points over the previous year, and to be 0.71 % in 2014. Examined quarterly, P_I is anticipated to be 0.20 and 0.26 % in the last two quarters in 2013, and to be 0.93, 0.92, 0.52 and 0.46 % in the four quarters of 2014, respectively.

The GDP deflator (P_GDP) is anticipated to fall to 0.83 % in 2013, a decrease of 1.11 percentage points, and to rise to 2.65 % in 2014 over the previous year. Examined quarterly, P_GDP is anticipated to be 0.69 and 0.37 % in the last two quarters of 2013, and 2.37 and 2.40 % in the first quarter and the fourth quarter of 2014 respectively, as shown in Fig. 3.6.

In sum, growth in China is anticipated to continuing decline, as domestic excess production capacity and weak external demand. The target of a growth of 7.5 % set by the central government could be reached though facing many challenges. Precautions or policy-adjustment will be needed to remedy these challenges. Policy makers should adjust macroeconomic policies in advance according to the dynamics of economic development, to ensure robust and stable growth.

Moreover, there is no significant risk of inflation in the next 2 years.

## *3.3.3 Forecasts of the Growth Rates of Other Major Macroeconomic Indicators*

### 3.3.3.1 Export, Import and Reserve Growth

The prospect of exports and imports of China will be weaker because of declining external demand. CQMM forecasts that the volume of exports at current price will rise by 7.4 % in 2013, a decrease of 0.54 percentage points over the previous year, while the volume of imports at current price will rise by 5.67 % in 2013, an increase of 1.31 percentage points over the previous year (Table 3.1). Examined quarterly, the year on year growth rate of exports will reach 2 year bottom in the first quarter of 2014, and then rise rapidly, while the growth rate of imports will be similar but more moderate. In particular, the growth rate of processing trade export is anticipated to be 0.8 %, while 8.87 % for general trade export. The foreign exchange reserve is anticipated to increase by 8.52 % for 2013 (Fig. 3.7). However, a softer growth of exports and imports for 2014 is expected, although growth of foreign exchange reserve in 2014 is anticipated to be slightly higher over 2013 (Table 3.1). What's more, the proportion of net exports in GDP is anticipated to be 3.08 and 3.12 % in 2013 and 2014, respectively.

#### 3.3.3.2 The Growth Rate of Total Fixed Capital Formation

In the second half of 2013, growth of infrastructure investment is anticipated to rise, in order to promote urbanization and maintain the economic growth rate at a reasonable range. CQMM indicates that growth of the total fixed capital formation at constant price would be 11.2 % in 2013, a rise of 2.97 percentage points over the previous year (Fig. 3.8). In 2014, the total fixed capital formation at constant price is expected to expand by 10.16 %. The urban total fixed capital formation at current price is expected to decrease to 16.29 % in 2014, from 20.38 % in 2013.

Examined quarterly, the year on year growth rate of total fixed capital formation at constant price will keep growing until the third quarter of 2013, reaching whole year high of 14.52 %, and then return to 12.55 % in last quarter of 2013.

Moreover, the year on year growth rate of urban total fixed capital formation at current price will fall to 17.28 % in the third quarter of 2013 but soon recover to 23.4 % in next quarter, and then keep steady for all quarters of 2014.

In addition, the total fixed capital formation may expand by 21.36 % in 2013, 2.04 percentage points higher than expansion in last year, and 18.56 % in 2014. Specifically, investment financed by the domestic loan and credits is likely to expand by 16.95 %, while investment from firms' self-financing by 20.86 %, and investment from other source by 31.12 % in 2013. In 2014, investment financed by the domestic loan and credits may grow by 14.99 %, while investments from firms' self-financing and other source will increase by 21.35 % and 13.88 % respectively (Table 3.2).

#### 3.3.3.3 The Growth Rate of Consumption

In terms of constant price, resident consumption will grow by 6.78 % in 2013, a decrease of 1.16 % over the previous year. The growth rate of retail sales of consumer goods at current price is expected to decrease from 14.14 % in 2012 to 13.12 % in 2013. In 2014, these two indicators will recover to 7.01 % and 14.14 % respectively.

**Table 3.1** Forecast of the growth rates of exports and imports in 2013–2014 (Unit: %)

| Time | Exports | | | | Imports | | | | The proportion of net exports in GDP |
|---|---|---|---|---|---|---|---|---|---|
| | At constant price | At current price | General trade at current price | Processing trade at current price | At constant price | At current price | General trade at current price | Processing trade at current price | |
| **2013** | **8.34** | **7.40** | **8.87** | **0.80** | **9.02** | **5.67** | **7.88** | **2.63** | **3.08** |
| Q1 | 18.16 | 18.09 | 16.30 | 3.41 | 10.36 | 8.07 | 0.10 | 9.24 | 4.30 |
| Q2 | 4.16 | 3.55 | 4.63 | −5.31 | 9.02 | 5.23 | 5.89 | −0.14 | 2.92 |
| Q3 | 6.68 | 5.89 | 7.83 | 5.61 | 9.48 | 6.44 | 12.15 | 4.40 | 2.62 |
| Q4 | 4.96 | 2.78 | 7.39 | −0.09 | 7.31 | 3.06 | 13.58 | −2.66 | 2.56 |
| **2014** | **6.82** | **4.57** | **8.01** | **4.82** | **5.65** | **3.14** | **7.27** | **2.03** | **3.12** |
| Q1 | −1.66 | −3.83 | 4.01 | −1.28 | 3.70 | −0.51 | 11.14 | −5.38 | 2.99 |
| Q2 | 7.34 | 4.55 | 6.93 | 7.45 | 5.29 | 3.05 | 6.80 | 6.48 | 2.97 |
| Q3 | 10.50 | 8.25 | 9.53 | 6.21 | 6.04 | 3.93 | 4.91 | 2.46 | 3.32 |
| Q4 | 11.54 | 9.85 | 11.49 | 7.21 | 7.50 | 6.09 | 6.52 | 5.14 | 3.18 |

Source: The researchers computed

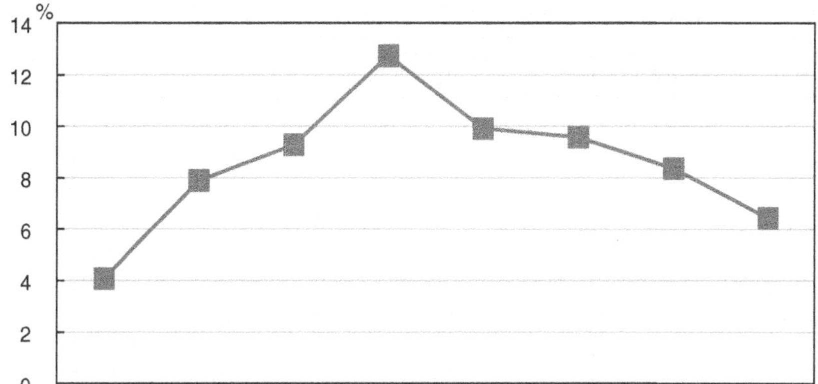


| | 2013Q1 | 2013Q2 | 2013Q3 | 2013Q4 | 2014Q1 | 2014Q2 | 2014Q3 | 2014Q4 |
|---|---|---|---|---|---|---|---|---|
| FER | 4.08 | 7.90 | 9.28 | 12.75 | 9.91 | 9.58 | 8.36 | 6.44 |

**Fig. 3.7** The growth rate of reserve (on year-on-year basis)

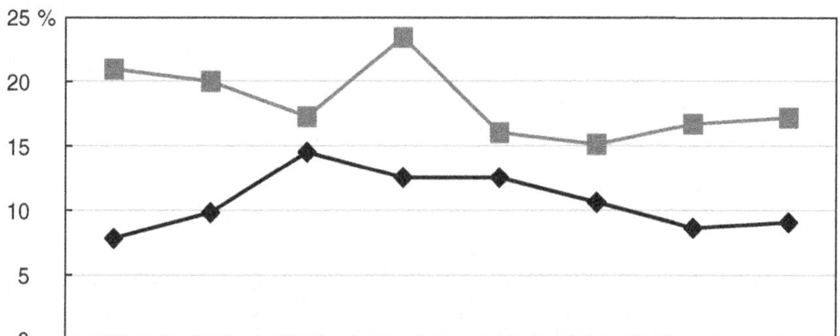


| | 2013Q1 | 2013Q2 | 2013Q3 | 2013Q4 | 2014Q1 | 2014Q2 | 2014Q3 | 2014Q4 |
|---|---|---|---|---|---|---|---|---|
| TI_C | 7.83 | 9.82 | 14.52 | 12.55 | 12.54 | 10.62 | 8.64 | 9.07 |
| FI_UR | 20.94 | 19.99 | 17.28 | 23.40 | 16.03 | 15.13 | 16.72 | 17.19 |

**Fig. 3.8** The growth rate of total fixed capital formation (on year-on-year basis) (Note: TI_C denotes the growth rate of total fixed capital formation at constant price while FI_UR denotes the growth rate of fixed capital formation in urban at current price)

The year on year growth rate of resident consumption at constant price will fluctuate all the time, reaching the lowest point of 2.4 % in the first quarter of 2014. Meanwhile, the year on year growth rate of retail sales of consumer goods at current price will climb all the way to the top of 14.68 % in the first quarter of 2014, and keep steady from then on (Fig. 3.9).

**Table 3.2** Forecast of the growth rate of investment in 2013–2014 (Unit: %)

| Time | Financed by the domestic loan and credits | From firms' self-financing | From other source | Total fixed capital formation |
|---|---|---|---|---|
| **2013** | **16.95** | **20.86** | **31.12** | **21.36** |
| Q1 | 10.95 | 16.65 | 42.37 | 19.53 |
| Q2 | 14.07 | 19.71 | 37.41 | 20.46 |
| Q3 | 15.77 | 22.30 | 22.08 | 19.01 |
| Q4 | 27.23 | 24.32 | 25.71 | 26.28 |
| **2014** | **14.99** | **21.35** | **13.88** | **18.56** |
| Q1 | 18.18 | 23.85 | 14.26 | 21.01 |
| Q2 | 15.06 | 22.78 | 12.66 | 18.74 |
| Q3 | 13.77 | 19.33 | 14.04 | 17.15 |
| Q4 | 13.29 | 19.89 | 14.54 | 17.63 |

Note: investment from other source is the fixed capital formation other than financed by the domestic loan and credits, financed by self and financed by foreign investment

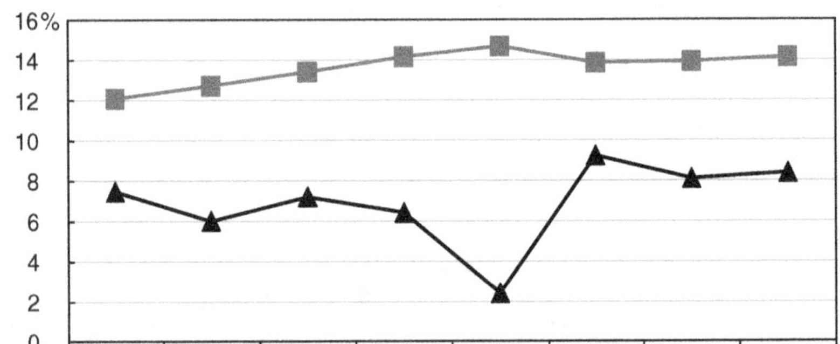


| | 2013Q1 | 2013Q2 | 2013Q3 | 2013Q4 | 2014Q1 | 2014Q2 | 2014Q3 | 2014Q4 |
|---|---|---|---|---|---|---|---|---|
| CON_D_C | 7.48 | 6.01 | 7.20 | 6.42 | 2.40 | 9.24 | 8.10 | 8.39 |
| RETAIL | 12.09 | 12.72 | 13.40 | 14.15 | 14.68 | 13.85 | 13.91 | 14.14 |

**Fig. 3.9** The growth rate of consumption (on year-on-year basis) (Note: CON_D_C denotes the growth rate of resident consumption and Retail denotes the growth rate of retail sales of consumer goods at current price)

### *3.3.4 Forecast of the Growth Rate of Government Revenue*

The government revenue in China will grow at a slowing pace, affected by the underperformance of manufacturing. The government revenue is anticipated to expand by 6.99 %, 6.09 percentage points less than growth in 2012, and be less than growth of GDP for the first time since 1997. Even in 2014, only a growth of 7.87 % can be expected. However, despite a slight setback in the first quarter of 2014, the year on year growth rate of government revenue will have an upward tendency in future (Fig. 3.10).

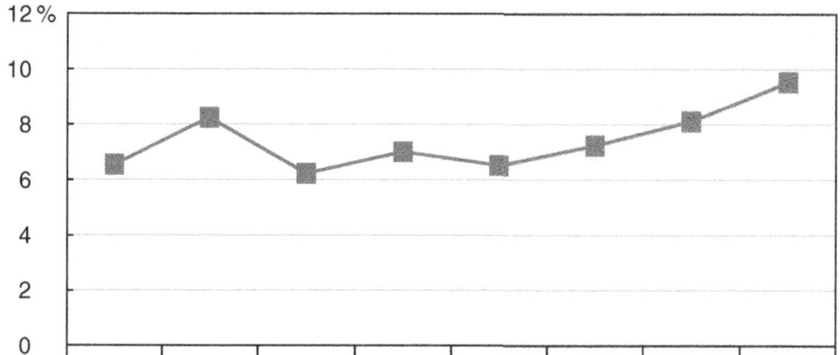


| | 2013Q1 | 2013Q2 | 2013Q3 | 2013Q4 | 2014Q1 | 2014Q2 | 2014Q3 | 2014Q4 |
|---|---|---|---|---|---|---|---|---|
| FISCAL_RE | 6.54 | 8.23 | 6.22 | 7.00 | 6.51 | 7.23 | 8.10 | 9.54 |

**Fig. 3.10** Forecast of government revenue growth rate (on year-on-year basis)

To conclude, the research team suggests as follows.

1. Growth in China will be more moderate in 2013, with regard to the impact from weak external demand and domestic excess production capacity. GDP is anticipated to rise by 7.54 % in 2013, a decrease of 0.26 percentage points than the previous year, while CPI is expected to remain at a relative low level of 2.45 % in 2013.
2. Although the global economy is restoring to grow, exports and imports of China will grow slowly in 2013. Residential consumption will grow slowly, because residential income will not increase significantly. Meanwhile, investment is still the mainspring of economic growth, especially taking account of the unbalanced economic structure. It is anticipated that investments in infrastructure and real estate will remain unchanged, and the growth rate of urban fixed assets investment will reach 20.38 %. It is not the best choice to drive growth through investment, but China has no choice except expanding investment, to prevent economy from falling.
3. Growth of government expenditure on people's wellbeing declined more rapidly than that on public administration, given slowing government revenue growth caused by underperformance of manufacturing. Declining in growth of fiscal expenditure as well as residences' real income will hamper the reforms of economic structure and rebalance of economy.

In the short run, investment would still drives growth in China, making it possible to defense downside risks by timely stimulus, especially when risks of inflation is expected to be low. However, in the long run, policy makers should pay more attention to management of supply side to increase growth potential. Furthermore, economic structure reforms are needed to ensure growth prospects in the long run, including fostering equally competitions, optimizing the allocation of resources, correcting the distortion of prices of factors, reducing the burden on enterprises and raising final consumption. Only in this way, can China gain more improvements.

# Chapter 4
# Policy Simulation

Since the global financial crisis of 2008, China's economy has entered a new period of development. The traditional pattern of economic growth, heavily relying on the exports and investment, could not continue, as the efficiency of economy has been declining. The credit loan increased sharply, and the investment in fixed assets grew smoothly with a slight increase since the first half of 2013. However, the growth rate of GDP was 7.7 % in the first quarter of 2013, of which only 2.3 percentage points was contributed by the gross capital formation, much lower than 4 percentage points during the last three quarters of 2012. It implied that the growth potential is nearly exhausted under current condition and the economic growth based on investment-driven strategy could not continue. Moreover, the efficiency of investment has declined and the relationship between the investment and economic growth has weakened. Although there was plenty of liquidity and the total amount of social financing grew fast, the "money shortage" of the banking system occurred in the June of 2013. All the above shows that the existing bank management system is not in accord with the requirement of the social and economic development. Therefore, the policy makers need to start the reforms of banking and financial system to follow the market principle, which means that the government should be involved directly in the market less than before.

In the short term, the relative stable economic growth could be realized by the proactive, timely and appropriate operations of macroeconomic policy. However, in the long term, the emphasis of macroeconomic policy should be placed on the production side of real economy, and on the stability and recovery of growth potential by deepening social and economic reform comprehensively and improving effective supply. The Eighteenth Report of Party says that: "deepening reform is the key to the transformation of economic development, and the core issue of economic reform is how to deal with the relationship between the market and

Center for Macroeconomic Research of Xiamen University, *China's Macroeconomic Outlook*, Current Chinese Economic Report Series, DOI 10.1007/978-3-642-54221-3_4,

government with more respects on the market and better understand of the role of government in the market."[1]

The ratio of government revenue to GDP is one of the keys for handling well the relationship between the market and government. How to collect and use the government revenue plays an important role in the social development. This made it possible for the people to learn more about how the government functions, and thus more effectively oversee its operations. If there are no law-based governments, there would be no order of market economy; moreover, if there are no efficient governments, there would be no healthy market economy. It is necessary to develop the socialist market economy through further social and economic reforms, such as to regulate and oversight the government behaviors, to control the scale of government revenue, and to make the government budget transparent and over-sighted by the public. Because of the slowdown of economic growth in the first half of 2013, which led to a lower growth of the government revenue than that of GDP, the problem about how to balance the market and government is even more severe. As the growth of government revenue slowed down, the balance of budget has worsened. Although the Ministry of Finance and State Taxation Administration has repeatedly stated "the administrations should resolutely stop taxing excessively", there are still many local governments focusing on the growth of government revenue to counterbalance the economic cycles, such as "excessive taxes", "trivial taxes" and even illegal charges.[2]

Therefore, this report is focused on regulating the government's operations behavior in collecting revenue as well as controlling the share of government revenue in GDP in order to investigate their macroeconomic effects by the policy simulation.

Before policy simulation, first introduce some backgrounds about the condition of the government revenue in China.

1. After the revenue-sharing reform in 1994, the government revenue in China has grown rapidly. During 1997–2012, the average annual growth rate of government revenue was 5.5 percentage points higher than that of GDP. As a result, the share of government revenue in GDP rose rapidly in the recent years (Fig. 4.1).

   The government revenue accounted for approximately 11.1 % of GDP in 1997; and this ratio rose to 22.6 % in 2012, an annual increase of about 0.77 percentage points averagely. According to the forecast of the CQMM, the growth rate of GDP in 2013 would reach 7.54 %, and the growth rate of government revenue would decrease to 6.99 %. As a net effect, the ratio of government

[1] "Firmly March on the Path of Socialism with Chinese Characteristics and Strive to Complete The Building of a Moderately Prosperous Society in All Respects, Report to the Eighteenth National Congress of the Communist Party of China" By Hu Jintao, page 20, People's publishing house, November, 2012.

[2] http://business.sohu.com/20130725/n382549987.shtml; http://business.sohu.com/20130802/n383179796.shtml; http://business.sohu.com/20130803/n383287072.shtml

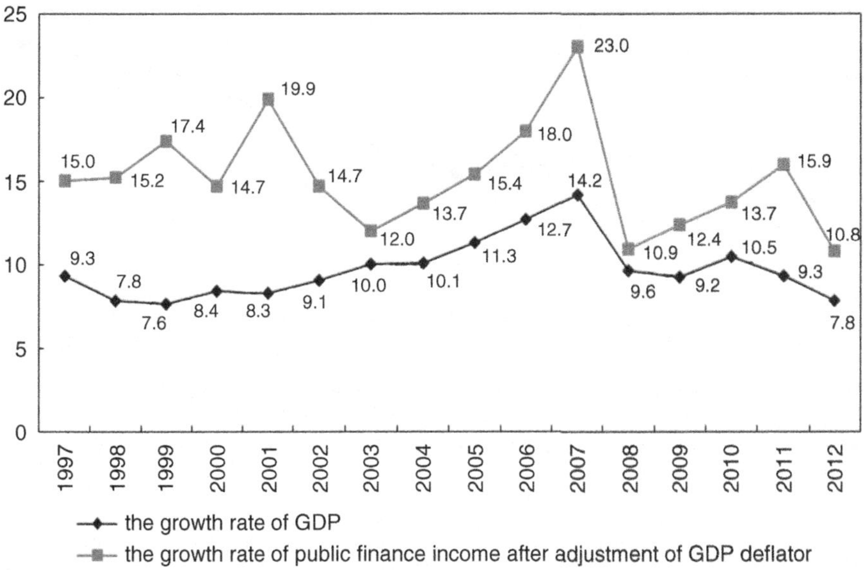


**Fig. 4.1** The growth rates of government revenue and GDP from 1997 to 2012 (Data Source: CEIC)

revenue in GDP in 2013 would probably decline slightly, 0.1 percentage points down compared with the previous year.

2. The share of government revenue in GDP has been too high. From 2010 to 2012, it was 34.4 %, 36.0 % and 36.0 % respectively.[3] According to the governments finance statistics published by IMF in 2010, the share of government revenue in GDP in China was much higher than in the developed countries, such as the United States, South Korea and Singapore. Considering the poor social welfare enjoyed by Chinese the general tax burden on the residents of China may be among the highest in the world.
3. Examining the composition of government revenue, we could find that the tax revenue shared by the local governments has been declining sharply since the revenue-sharing reform in 1994. In order to have enough revenue to meet the needs of their own expenses, the local governments are very enthusiastic in collecting income by the means other than the taxes, including the non-tax revenue, general fund revenue, social contribution income, operating income of state owned capital. In addition, we could also find that the ratio of non-tax revenue in government revenue gradually rose year by year: 5.4 % in 1994 and14.2 % in 2012 which was 8.8 percentage points higher (Fig. 4.2). From 2008 to 2012, averagely 80 % of China's non-tax revenue was collected by the

[3] It did not include the retained profits of SOEs nor the loans obtained by all levels of governments through various financing platforms (this also led to a increasingly serious debt problems of local governments in recent years).

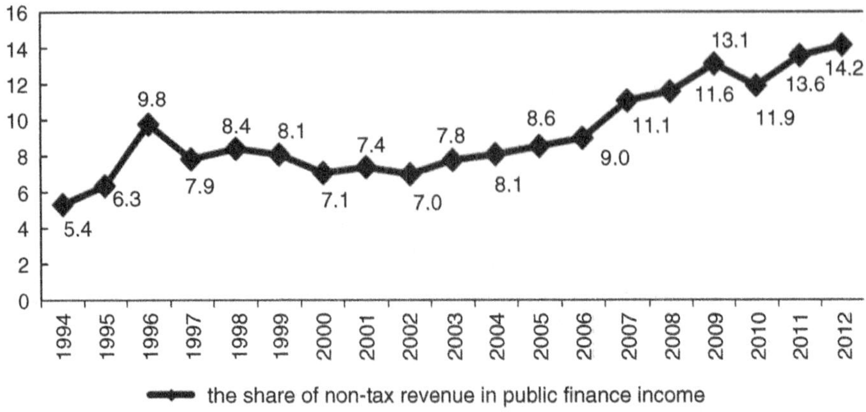


**Fig. 4.2** The shares of non-tax revenue in government revenue from 1994 to 2012 (Data Source: CEIC)

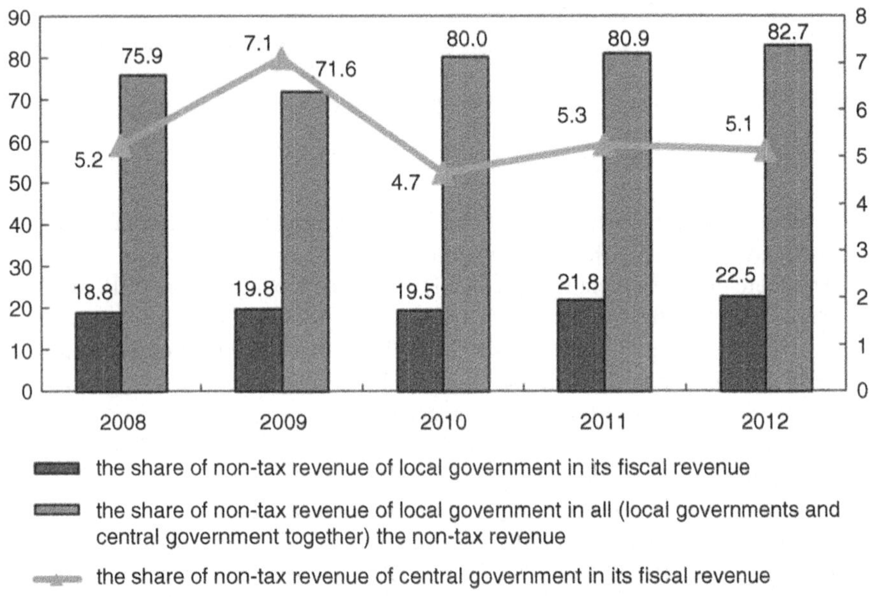


**Fig. 4.3** The shares of non-tax revenue in government revenue of the central and local governments (Note: the *right axis* is according to the share of non-tax revenue in government revenue of the central government. Data Source: CEIC Data)

local governments, 20 % of which was collected by central government. On the other hand, the ratio of non-tax revenue to total revenue was 20 % for the local governments, while the non-tax revenue accounted for only 5 % of the central government revenue (Fig. 4.3).

Turning to the composition of non-tax revenue, the special revenue, administrative fees, confiscated revenue and other revenue accounted for approximately

20.6 %, 29.3 %, 11.3 % and 38.8 % respectively from 2007 to 2012; Compared with the tax revenue, the non-tax revenue has such features as non-standard, non-transparent, injustice, inequality and much more arbitrarily dominated by the local governments. The increasing proportion of non-tax revenue results in such outcome as follows:

1. It increases the financial burden of the enterprises, especially SMEs (small and medium enterprises), as well as the residents;
2. Because the non-tax revenue is collected quite arbitrarily, it leads to a strong unpredictability, and extra operating cost of the social or economic agents, both of which would reduce the efficiency of enterprises and undermine the resident consumption and economic growth;
3. It would easily lead to illegal administration, and is corruption-prone. In order to establish and improve the socialist market economy, we must improve the relationship between the market and government, control the revenue and expenditure of the government, regulate the government operations and behaviors and implement the effective restraint and oversight on the government budget by the public.

Thus, the research team focuses on the effects on the economic growth and structure adjustment of controlling the growth of government revenue specially on compressing the non-tax revenue and reducing the financial burden on the enterprises, especially the SMEs, and the residents.

## 4.1 The Policy Simulation Designs

In order to simulate the macroeconomic effects of controlling the government revenue growth and regulating the government's operations or behaviors for collecting revenue, the research team assumes:

1. If the share of government non-tax revenue to government revenue had dropped to 10 % during 2007–2012, and then the government non-tax revenue would have decreased by 63.07, 108.17, 238.32, 175.62, 416.51 and 545.99 billion Yuan respectively.
2. At the same time, the reduced part of government non-tax revenue above could be transferred to enterprises or workers to increase the profits or wages.

Based on the assumptions made above, the research team designs two scenarios as follows:

In the first scenario, all the reduced non-tax revenue would be transferred to enterprises to increase their profit;

In the second scenario, all the reduced part of government non-tax revenue would be transferred to employees to increase their wages.

The economic reasons behind such policy simulation are as following: reducing non-tax revenue has negative as well as positive effects on economic growth.

The simulation would find out the net effect. On one hand, decreasing non-tax revenue would reduce the government revenue, thus lead to a tight public finance expense which might undermine the growth of GDP. On the other hand, the reduced non-tax revenue would be transferred to the enterprises or residents, leading to an ease of tax burden on the enterprises, which were equivalent to increasing their profit or reducing their operating costs, therefore the enterprises could expand the investment with more self-raised fund; the improvement of resident income would promote their consumption; In either way, reducing the government non-tax revenue and transferring it to the enterprises of worker could stimulate the economic growth.

Through the upgrading CQMM, the research team would simulate the impacts of decreasing the non-tax revenue ratio on the GDP growth, on the economic structure adjustment and on the share of government revenue in GDP.

## 4.2 The Policy Simulation Results

### *4.2.1 The First Scenario: All the Reduced Non-tax Revenue Would Be Transferred to Enterprises to Increase Their Profit*

If the reduced non-tax revenue was transferred to the enterprises, then the simulation results based on CQMM show that:

1. The growth rate of GDP would decrease a little, and the aggregate production gap or the output gap would become larger slightly;
2. Considering the components of GDP based on the expenditures accounting approach, the share of resident consumption would be nearly the same, the share of gross fixed capital formation would rise slightly, implying that the macroeconomic structure would be basically unchanged;
3. The growth rate of tax revenue would increase after decreasing at the very beginning, which could compensate the declining of the growth of government revenue; the proportion of government revenue in GDP would slightly drop. The details are specifically listed as follows:

   First, to reduce the non-tax revenue and to transfer the reduced part of government non-tax revenue to the enterprises would slow down the growth of GDP slightly. During the 3 years of simulation of 2010–2012, the growth rate of GDP would rise instead of falling in 2010, an increase of 0.05 percentage points compared with the baseline model which were to run the regression model of CQMM without changing any exogenous conditions; during 2011 and 2012, the growth rate of GDP would decrease 0.03 and 0.1 percentage points than the baseline model respectively (Fig. 4.4). According to these effects, the aggregate production gap or output gap would decrease 0.04 percentage points in 2010, and then slightly expand, with an increase of 0.01 percentage points in 2012.

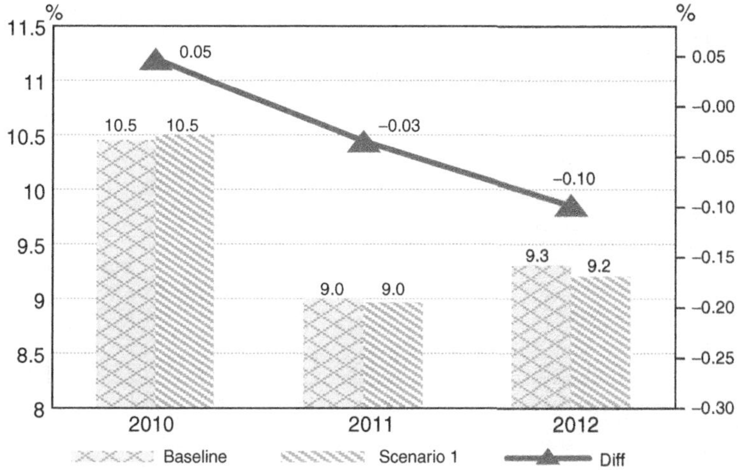


**Fig. 4.4** The growth rates of GDP in baseline model and the first scenario (Note: Baseline (*left axis*) denotes the growth rate of GDP in the baseline model; Scenario 1 (*left axis*) denotes the counterpart in the first scenario; Diff (*right axis*) denotes the difference between the two results above)

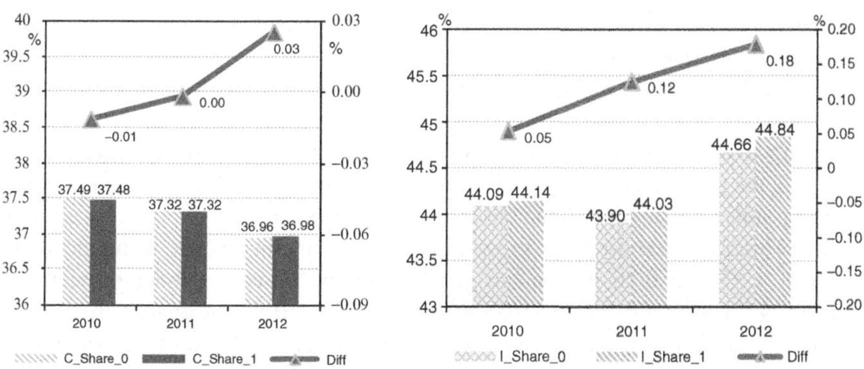


**Fig. 4.5** The changes of composition of GDP under the expenditure method (Note: C_Share_0 and C_Share_1 denote the shares of resident consumption in GDP in the baseline model and the first scenario; I_Share_0 and I_Share_1 denote the shares of gross fixed capital formation in GDP in the baseline model and the first scenario; Diff denotes the difference between the two results above)

Secondly, the macroeconomic structure would be essentially unchanged. From 2010 to 2012, the share of residential consumption in GDP was basically unchanged in the simulation; the share of gross fixed capital formation in GDP would slightly increase, specially, an increase of 0.05, 0.12 and 0.18 percentage points respectively. (Fig. 4.5)

Thirdly, because the reduction of non-tax revenue would increase the profit of enterprises, the growth of enterprises' self-raised investment would improve

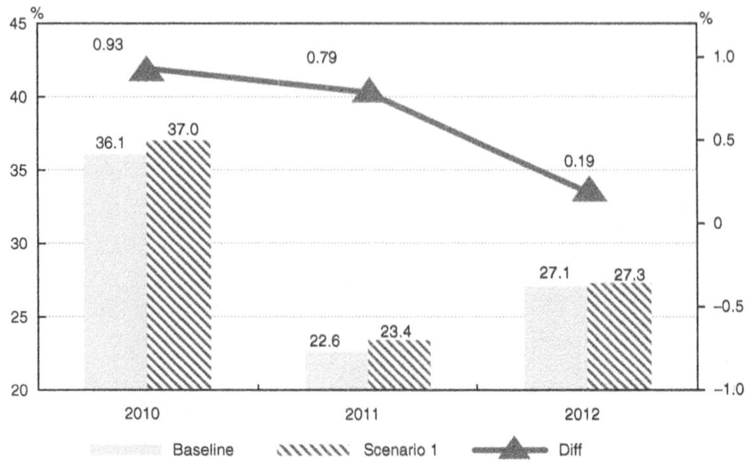


**Fig. 4.6** The growth rates of investment by corporate self-raised fund (Note: Baseline denotes the growth rate of investment by corporate self-raised fund in the baseline model; Scenario 1 denotes the counterpart in the first scenario; Diff denotes the difference between the two results above)

greatly than the baseline model. From 2010 to 2012, the growth of enterprises' self-raised investment would increase 0.93, 0.79 and 0.19 percentage points respectively (Fig. 4.6).

Fourthly, although the improvement of growth of investment from enterprises' self-raised fund drives the growth of GDP as well as tax revenue, the changes of growth of government revenue are somewhat different. From 2010 to 2012, the growth rate of tax revenue would change −4.63, 0.64 and 0.54 percentage points compared with the baseline model respectively, which shows a rising trend after the first drop; the growth rate of government revenue would decrease 2.33, 1.97 and 0.26 percentage points than the baseline model respectively (Fig. 4.7). The ratio of government revenue in GDP would change to 19.9 %, 20.6 % and 21.1 % respectively, a decrease of 0.41, 0.76 and 0.81 percentage points compared with the baseline model (Fig. 4.8).

### 4.2.2 *The Second Scenario: All the Reduced Part of Government Non-tax Revenue Would be Transferred to Employees to Increase Their Wages*

If the reduced part of government non-tax revenue would be transferred to employees to increase their wages during 2007–2012, then the simulation results based on CQMM shows that:

1. The growth rate of GDP would slightly increase, and the aggregate production gap or output gap would narrow evidently;

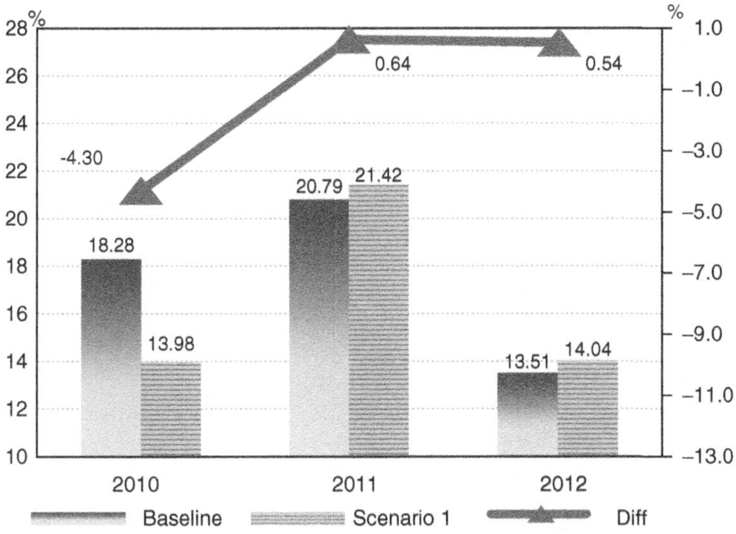


**Fig. 4.7** The growth rates of tax revenue. Note: Baseline denotes the growth rate of tax revenue in the baseline model; Scenario 1 denotes the counterpart in the first scenario; Diff denotes the difference between the two results above)

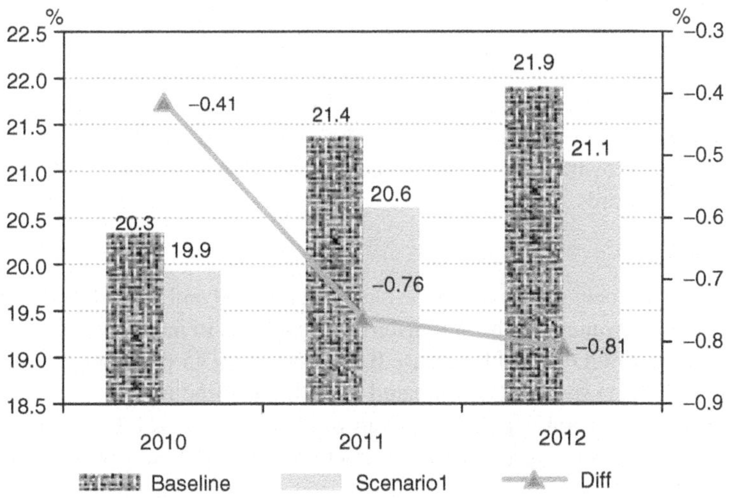


**Fig. 4.8** The shares of government revenue in GDP. Note: Baseline denotes the share of government revenue in the baseline model; Scenario 1 denotes the counterpart in the first scenario; Diff denotes the difference between the two results above

2. Considering the components of GDP based on the expenditures accounting approach, the share of residential consumption would significantly increase, while the share of gross fixed capital formation would slightly decrease. Hence, the macroeconomic structure could be improved;

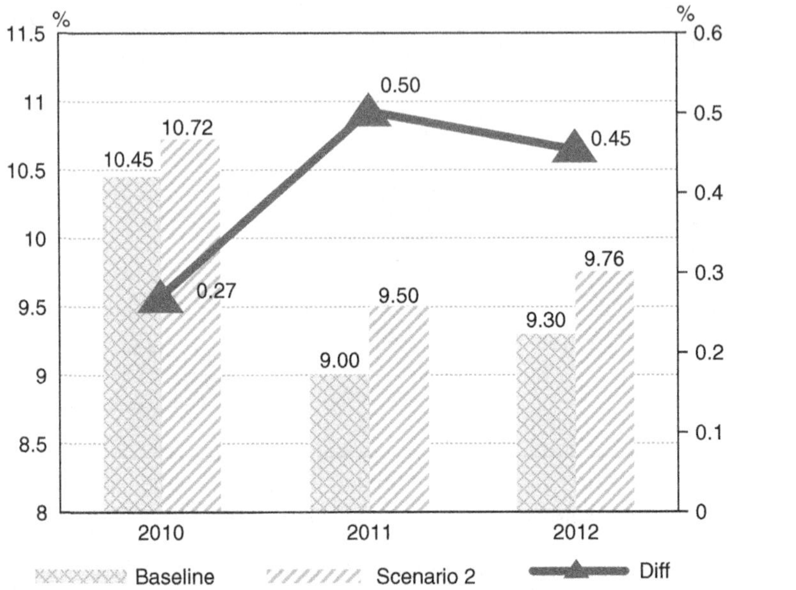


**Fig. 4.9** The growth rates of GDP (Note: Baseline denotes the growth rates of GDP in the baseline model; Scenario 2 denotes the counterpart in the second scenario; Diff denotes the difference between the two results above)

3. The growth of tax revenue would be slightly fast, and the decreasing trend of the growth of government revenue would be more moderate; however, due to the more rapid growth of GDP, the share of government revenue in GDP would decrease forwards.

In summary:

Firstly, if government non-tax revenue had been reduced and the reduced part of the government revenue had been transferred to workers to increase their wages, the growth rate of GDP would increase 0.27, 0.50 and 0.45 percentage points from 2010 to 2012, respectively, compared with the baseline model. Meanwhile, the aggregate production gap or output gap would decrease 0.24, 0.70 and 1.13 percentage points, so that the excess production capacity would weaken gradually (Fig. 4.9).

Secondly, the imbalances of economic structure could be corrected to some degree. From 2010 to 2012, the share of resident consumption in GDP would have significantly risen, with an increase of 0.09, 0.28 and 0.47 percentage points respectively; the share of gross fixed capital formation in GDP would have decreased by 0.15, 0.42 and 0.66 percentage points respectively (Fig. 4.10).

Thirdly, due to the expansion of resident consumption and the acceleration of the economic growth, the growth of investment by enterprises' self-raised fund would have increased more in the second scenario than in the baseline model.

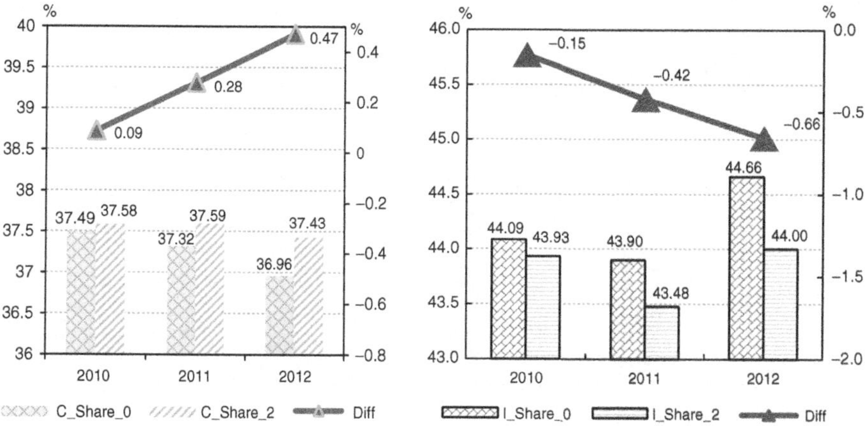


**Fig. 4.10** The expenditure structure of GDP (Note: C_Share_0 and C_Share_2 denote the ratio of resident consumption in GDP in the baseline model and the second scenario respectively; I_Share_0 and I_Share_2 denote the ratio of gross fixed capital formation in GDP in the baseline model and the second scenario; Diff denote the difference between the ratios in the baseline model and the second scenario)

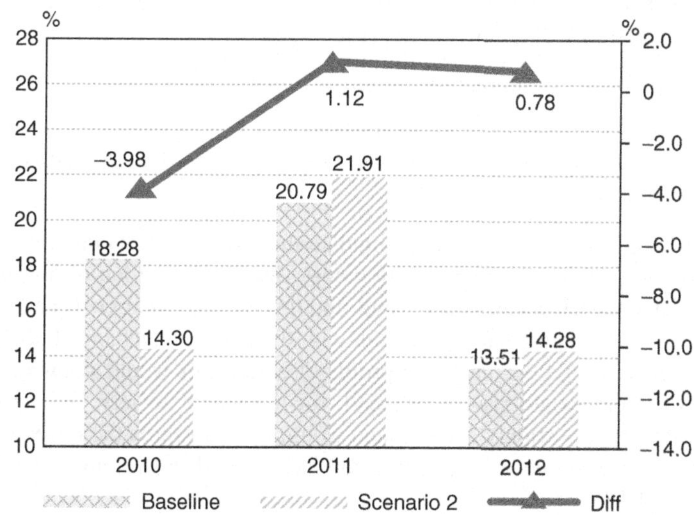


**Fig. 4.11** The growth rates of tax revenue (Note: Baseline denotes the growth rate of tax revenue in the baseline model; Scenario 2 denotes the counterpart in the second scenario; Diff denotes the difference between the two rates above)

At the same time, the growth of tax revenue would have gradually accelerated. Compared to the baseline model, the growth rate of tax revenue would first decrease 3.98 percentage points, and then increase 1.12 and 0.78 percentage points respectively during 2010–2012 (Fig. 4.11). The share of government

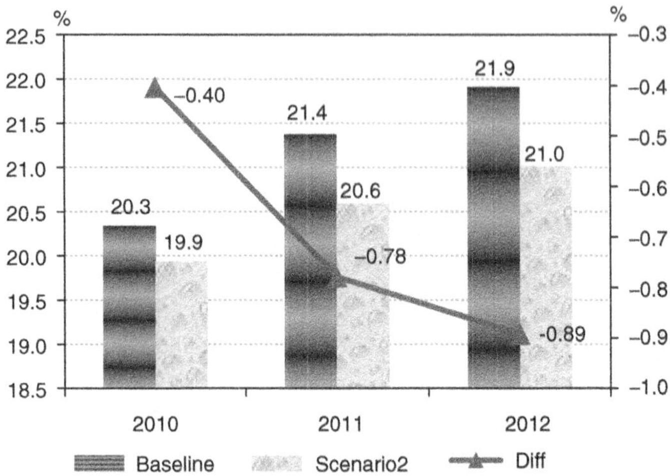


**Fig. 4.12** The shares of government revenue in GDP. Note: Baseline denotes the share of government revenue in the baseline model; Scenario 2 denotes the counterpart in the second scenario; Diff denote the difference between the two ratios above

revenue in GDP would have decreased 0.4, 0.78 and 0.89 percentage points respectively during the same period (Fig. 4.12).

The results of policy simulation above show that:

1. The effect of reducing the non-tax revenue of the enterprises on economy is not significant, which seems contrary to the economic intuition. We believe that the reasons may be as follows:

   (a) The CQMM is still unable to simulate the effects of reducing non-tax revenue of government on production cost: decreasing burden of non-tax revenue somewhat means decreasing enterprises' marginal cost, and it would promote the aggregate production with the demand unchanged, the price of products would decrease, the profits of enterprises would improve, and the investment would rise. In the end, for the whole society, the equilibrium point between supply and demand would move towards the lower right, and the excess production capacity would be digested and assimilated efficiently (Fig. 4.13).

   (b) The relief of non-tax burden would have led to an improvement of investment environment for the enterprises. As the production cost decreased, the enterprises would become more eager to investment with self-raised fund and then the investment would increase. The investment from the enterprises, which were based on the market expectation independently, would lead to a more effective supply. However, such effect could hardly be fully realized in the existing simulation system.

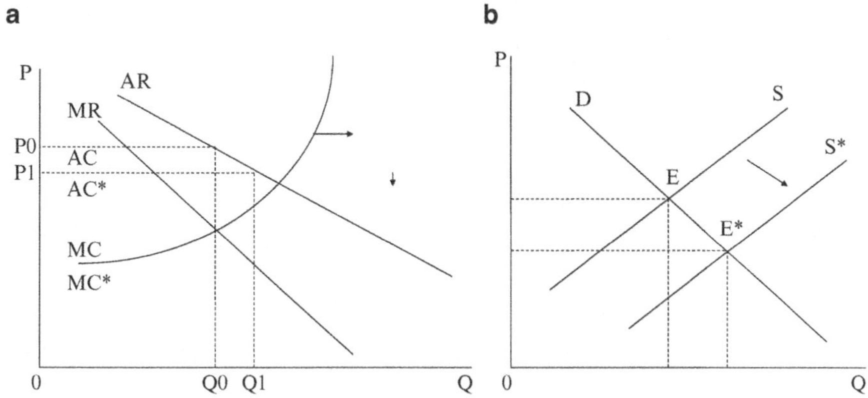


**Fig. 4.13** The effects of decreasing non-tax revenue on the decision of enterprise production. (**a**) Marginal cost of enterprise. (**b**) Change of supply and demand

(c) At present, the growth of resident income is slow, the resident consumption is low, and the excess production capacity remains. We could only simulate the impacts of decreasing the non-tax revenue from the enterprises on their self-raised investment in this model, but we could not simulate all the effects in the case of decreasing production cost. Although the simulation of decreasing of non-tax burden on the enterprises was not evident, we think that we could not deny the proactive role of decreasing non-tax burden on the improvement of economic environment and efficiency of enterprises.

2. In the case that the worker wage was low, if we could lower the non-tax burden on the enterprises and transfer it to employees to increase their wages; we believe that it would be effective for promoting the economic growth, narrowing the aggregate production gap or output gap, rebalancing the economic structure, expanding the resident consumption, stimulating investment in real economy, and increasing the tax revenue and so on.
3. Through standardizing the government's operations in exercising government power, the proposed non-tax revenue reduction policy would provide positive effect on China's economy. The results of policy simulation about the economic effects illustrate one fact: the share of government revenue in GDP in China has been too high, which is not conducive to the economic growth and structure adjustment, as well as the expansion of resident consumption.
4. In the case that the share of government revenue was too high, restricting and regulating the government operations and behaviors on collecting fiscal revenue will promote government administration in accordance with laws, rules and regulations, would enhance the openness and fairness of government management, improve market economy and form a clear expectation about the government behavior for the whole society.

# Chapter 5
# Policy Implications

## 5.1 Policy Implications and Suggestions

On the basis of forecast and simulation result above, our research team puts forward the following policy recommendations.

1. Although economic growth is slowing down, China still has a good chance to achieve the economic development target which is to increase GDP by 7.5 % and to keep price level stable. While macroeconomic policy authority should always keep an eye on economic trends home and abroad, take precautions and measures to carry out timely and appropriate anticipatory adjustments and fine-tuning to ensure the realization of economic growth target.
2. The reason that the growth rate of government revenue falls this year mainly lies in economic slowdown and economic system adjustment, but it still is higher than 7.5 % because that structure of government revenue has not substantially changed. Moreover, this is an opportunity to reform the revenue system. It should begin with transformation of the pattern of economic development and adjustment of economic structure, then take advantage of the opportunity to reduce the fiscal expenditure and adjust structure of fiscal expenditures.
3. It's impossible that government revenue grows faster than the economy for a long period, and overhigh proportion of the government revenue will seriously impede the development of market economy. Therefore, it's essential to control the growth rate and proportion of government revenue in GDP, to standardize sources of revenue and government administration in collecting revenue through economic system adjustment. On the other hand, it's also essential to reduce the share of non-tax revenue in government revenue gradually, to adjust structure of fiscal expenditures, to ensure that expenditures on people's wellbeing grow steadily and to reduce cost of general public service.
4. To improve socialist market economy, it should be a long-term trend that fiscal revenue increases in line with economic growth. So government must be low-cost in the long run as well as in the short run, it should be carried out to streamline

Center for Macroeconomic Research of Xiamen University, *China's Macroeconomic Outlook*, Current Chinese Economic Report Series, DOI 10.1007/978-3-642-54221-3_5,

government departments at all levels and establish small government. In addition, strengthening administrative and budgetary oversight by the public is needed.

5. Reducing non-tax revenue and standardizing government administration of collecting revenue can lower the proportion of government revenue. It's helpful to reduce government revenue and thus reduce the proportion of government revenue in GDP, and at the same time it is advantageous to promote administration in accordance with laws, rules and regulations, enhance the transparency and fairness of government management, promote formulation of normal market economy order, and help participants in the market to formulate consistent expectation towards government administration. Most of non-tax revenue is collected by local governments, and this phenomenon exists mainly because of the unreasonable fiscal system, especially the revenue system. We should reform fiscal system and adjust the economic rights and duties between central government and local governments, and strive to match the rights and duties. Both central and local initiative should be brought into play with clear responsibility of each party.
6. Special attention should be paid to areas which are important to the people's wellbeing such as education, scientific technology, culture and recreation, medical and health care, social security and employment, and the government should prevent expenditure decline sharply in these areas. To reduce government overhead, we should strictly control the construction and expansion of government office buildings, truly standardize official entertaining, and plug up loopholes in management rules by banning the construction of more luxury government building and halls with excuses of people's wellbeing program or using some fabricated titles such as "civil service center ". We suggest that government should adjust statistical classification of public expenditure, distinguish administrative expenditure and service expenditure on people's wellbeing clearly, and this suggestion is advantageous to auditing and oversight from higher authorities and the public, and is also helpful to reduce the administrative cost and establish a service-oriented government.

China's economic development since the global financial crisis (specially from this year) has shown some new characteristics as follows: facing with uncertainties abroad and at home, China's development potential under current economic system is experiencing a downward pressure and the investment-driven pattern of economic growth is not sustainable. The efficiency of investment drops down, thus the tie between investment and economic growth becomes loose. Apparently, if we don't further deepen all-round reform in social economic system, develop and improve socialist market economy, release economic development potential and start a new engine for economic development as soon as possible, the decline of economic growth due to economic structural imbalance will continue. Our research team suggests that stabilizing potential growth rate is possible essentially by further deepening reform in social economic reform, expanding effective supply, enhancing efficiency of investment, and thus raising labor productivity. Therefore, we must trigger a new round of reform in social and economic system, develop and improve socialist market economy further, promote to compete on an equal basis, explore space of resource optimization, correct the distortion of relative prices of factors, adjust economic structure, improve government public administration, lighten the burden on enterprises, enhance efficiency of supply, release economic development potential and foster domestic demand. The new round overall reform in social economic system will not only expand China's economic development space tremendously, maintain steady growth of China's economy, but also become an institutional guarantee for transferring the pattern of economic development, transition from a middle-income economy to a higher stage.

[illegible]

# Appendices

## Appendix 1: Comments and Discussions

August 18, Xiamen University and the Economic Information Daily in Beijing jointly held a "Financial Restructuring and Improve – Efficiency on Economic Development – High Level Symposium on China's Economy and Press Conference of China's Quarterly Macroeconomic Model (CQMM) Forecast". The participating experts and scholars expressed their views on the current economic situation and prospects, and put forward relevant policy recommendations.

1. **Professor Xu Xianchun, Vice director of National Bureau of Statistics of China**

   There are five characteristics of current economic situation:

Firstly, China's economy is experiencing steady growth at present. The growth rate of economy ranged from 7.4 to 7.9 % for the last five quarters, which shows the relatively steady growth tendency; gross fixed capital formation develops in a stable way, industrial added value also experiences a steady growth, residents' consumption slipped slightly; the contribution net exports makes to economic growth has switched to be positive this year rather than negative last year.

Secondly, the growth rate of industries and enterprises' profit is lower and there's an obvious divergent trend. The minority of industries offers up the majority of new profits, the majority of industries just offered up less profit. And some companies of industries with excess production capacity still have a good performance.

Thirdly, commercial housing sales market fluctuates wildly. Both sold space of commercial housing and sales of commercial housing increased a lot at the beginning of this year and then began to drop.

Fourthly, per capita disposable income of urban residents and per capita cash income of rural residents both present the trend that the growth rates drop quarterly. And the reason that urban per capita disposable income grows slowly lies in that the growth rate of high-income group's income falls. But per capita average incomes

Center for Macroeconomic Research of Xiamen University, *China's Macroeconomic Outlook*, Current Chinese Economic Report Series, DOI 10.1007/978-3-642-54221-3, of urban and rural residents as a whole grows faster than GDP. The growth rates of per capita real income of rural residents and per capita disposable income of urban residents are 9.2 % and 6.5 % respectively in the first half of this year, and the growth rate of synthesized average incomes of urban and rural residents is higher than that of GDP, which is 7.6 %.

The last aspect goes to price index. Since producer price and import and export price fall, CPI keeps a steady and slight growth.

**2. Liu Shangxi, researcher from Research Institute for Fiscal Science, Ministry of Finance, P.R.China: Structural Reform of Public Finance, from a Perspective of Public Risk Management**

To sum up, there is three viewpoints about fiscal structural reform in public opinion. First, a massive tax cut is appealed, and tax burden at the macro-level is condemned to be so heavy that hampers economic growth. Second, a shortage of public services calls for more financial backing. Third, deficits and debts of governments, especially of local governments, are considered to be too high to be reduced. Looked at in isolation, these viewpoints are all reasonable, but there would be a contradiction when they are put together. Obviously, governments could not raise expenditure and cut tax without higher deficit. So the structural reform of public finance is essentially a series of trade-offs between different policy risks.

Policy risks in public finance, to some degree, are just financial risks, which are easy to control. But fiscal policy is one of main policy tools of governments in China and affects every aspect of economy, so it is needed to think about this topic from a perspective of public risk management.

Public risks China currently faces are all caused by development, including livelihood issues, structural imbalance, shortages of resources and pollution, which are risks of development regarding society, economy and environment respectively. To solve all these problems require long-term and overall planning more than makeshifts for short-term. However, the macroscopic control, which is highly prized now, is the later rather than the former.

To conclude, governments should change their macroscopic policy from readjustment and control to management and risks prevention, planning overall and for long term. Only in this way can the contradiction mentioned above be solved. For example, it is better to focus on improvement of human resource than of livelihood, form the perspective of macroscopic management. An accelerating accumulation of human resource will make the economy growing sustainably and people's livelihood better, finally reducing the risk of development. Meanwhile, tax cuts, especially for minor enterprises, can lower the threshold for starting a business and activate economy. Although tax cuts may lead to heaver financial pressure, it is beneficial in general. What's more, it is important to find the "sweet point" when handling deficits.

Still from this perspective, the risk of public finance is essentially a kind of fiscal policy tool, which converts the public risks to itself. This is something like a risk pool which makes the public risks quantized and controllable, while low cost and effective. In a word, the structural reform of public finance is to make the most use of this tool, and to manage the risks of development in China.

### 3. Zhang Liqun, Researcher from Development Research Center of the State Council: China's Economy Is Expected to Evolve at a Steady Pace

Growth in China is expected to keep steady, with a pace between 7 and 8 %. This forecast is due to two factors.

First, the domestic market demand becomes weaker, reflecting slower external demand growth resulting from global financial crisis and that the upgrading of consumption composed mainly of traveling and living costs is now limited by bottlenecks in urbanization. Urbanization in China is extensive and seriously interfered by administrative factors. Each level of government acts of its own free will, causing a lot of problems of imbalance and unsustainability. The omission of long-term planning and systematic supportive construction will heavily weigh on developments of the auto market and the housing market.

Second, the increases of factor costs make it impossible to maintain a low-cost expanding, so low-standard projects should be halted. China should pay more attention to the scale, technique standard and staff's professionalism of a project, to reduce the pressure of rising costs.

China is still in an upward process of industrialization and urbanization, and that means there would not be hard landing in China, although growth in recent periods moderates slightly. The weaker demand do not means an end of sustained and rapid growth, much less a constantly and long-term decline. However, the industrialization and urbanization in China are still developing rapidly. The still-low per capita GDP, which is 6,000 US dollar, depicts that there is a huge space for development.

In this context, policy makers in China should attach more importance not only to controlling downside risks bring by economic transform, but also to coordinating supply side policies and demand side policies. Only in this way, the multi-goal of establishing growth, improving economic transition and deepening reform can be reached, and the people's wellbeing can be achieved.

### 4. Li Xuesong, Vice Director of Institute of Quantitative & Technical Economics, Chinese Academy of Social Sciences

At first, I think policy simulation analysis is one of advantages of this report, but there are still some questions to be discussed further such as GDP growth rate, gross fixed capital formation, exports growth rate and a lack of compatibility of prediction data of year 2014.

Secondly, it's about this year's economic situation. On the whole, the economic development target which is to increase GDP by 7.5 % can be realized this year. The keynote of policy at the beginning of this year is to seek improvement in stability, and a new term "make an achievement in stability" is added recently, at the same time, a series of fine-tuning policies are carried out, including ten major steps. Many economic indicators in July present signs of economic rebound, such as steel price, automobile production and sales amount, real estate development and investment of shantytown renovation, in addition, railway infrastructure investment will grow faster in the second half of this year. From the point of indicators of July, some indicators pick up obviously, and other indicators are stabilizing, so there's a good start of the economy of third quarter. In addition, euro-zone economy of second quarter had been out of recession temporarily and enjoyed a quarter-on-quarter growth by 0.3 %, which is slightly higher than expectations. Although euro-zone economy is still weak, the growth rate of China's gross export this year is expected to be higher than that of last year.

Thirdly, to reform fiscal and taxation systems, it's necessary to transform structure, to increase the proportion of direct tax and decrease the proportion of indirect tax and to carry out the tax reduction and tax increase policy at the same time. Specifically, policy of the business tax reform to levy VAT is a kind of tax cuts, and government can further lower tax rates of VAT in the future, reduce the indirect tax and enhance the vitality of real economy. Meanwhile, central government should accelerate levying property tax, which provides local government a steady source of tax revenue. Housing property tax and other local taxes should be also important content of fiscal and taxation system reform. These flexible tax adjustments can keep the ratio of government revenue to GDP steady and facilitate to adjust income distribution.

5. **Zhang Xiaojing, Researcher and Director of the Office of the Department of Economics, Chinese Academy of Social Sciences: Innovate in Macro-control Mode**

First of all, for China's current macroeconomic situation, my opinions are as follows. Firstly, in July the improvement of monthly data does not represent changes in overall economic trends, need to observe for a longer period of time; secondly, economic growth is not likely to fall further; finally, there are many risks in the economy, including real estate, local debt, excess capacity, and so on. In addition, there are some arguments that of "China's high investment and low consumption is a Ponzi scheme" appearing on the current international scene, which does not accord with the actual Chinese economy. The large number of Chinese investment in infrastructure is able to benefit in the future.

Fully recognizing the current economic stage is the premise for implementing macro-control. With China's current economy is in the period of growth rate shifting, the throes of structural adjustment, the digestion period of stimulating policy in the early days, as well as the world economy is also in deep adjustment, the development environment is very complex. Based on such judgment, the macro-control should not only focus on this year or next year, whether to reach 7.5 or 7 %, but should have a long-term plan instead. The long term should be at least 10 years in power cycle (By convention is two terms).

Based on changes in the micro foundation of macro-control, it is needed adjustment that the basic mode of macro-control. Reforming and opening up for more than 30 years, the market economy system has been basically formed; the market mechanism plays a fundamental role in the allocation of resources. At the same time, the local government competition also makes the local impulse and enthusiasm cannot be ignored. Therefore, when implementing macro-control policies, to be able to think of the market response, the response of local governments. In some cases, the government does not move, the market moves; the central government does not move, local government moves. We must not act too hastily. This is the deep understanding of the micro foundation for macro-control.

Insist on the bottom line of thinking of macro-control. This includes three aspects: (1) the social bottom line. Namely, the macro policy should be steady, micro policy to live, social policy to support. (2) the bottom line of the growth. In the reasonable interval of the growth, we should emphasize the upper limit, the lower limit and the bottom line, in order to ensure that build a well-off society in an all-round way by 2020, achieve the goal of doubling GDP in 2010, the average annual growth rate of GDP reach at least 6.5 % above in the next few years, the bottom line of economic growth set at 7 %. (3) the bottom line of financial risk. In terms of financial risk, we should prevent the emergence of regional and systemic risks, and that is the bottom line.

The direction of macro-control policy shift from demand management to supply management. For example, the urbanization problem which we emphasize is the potential for expanding domestic demand and the reference itself is no problem, but if we only emphasize the demand, rather than improve the efficiency from the supply side, the urbanization will be a disaster. The problem of excess production capacity also followed the way of demand management in the past, but in fact, the excess capacity has been mostly caused by supply-side factors, such as some industrial policy as well as local redundant construction. The essence of emphasizing supply management is to deepen reform, and rationalize the system and mechanism of the supply side.

### 6. Professor Liu Xiahui, the Chief Researcher of the Economic Growth Research Department in the Institute of Economic Research, the Chinese Academy of Social Sciences

The macroeconomic policy should focus on the supply side rather than the demand side.

I think that it could not completely solve the economic problem only by using demand management policy under the current background that the growth potential has not been realized. Therefore, we need to enhance the macroeconomic management to improve the supply efficiency. The main content should include the followings the labor and capital input, and the social benefit could be realized better as the combination of supply factors could be improved efficiently.

The current policies are always beneficial for some people in the market rather than the whole market participants, accordingly it lead to special bottlenecks in the market. As there was free lunch, or arbitrage, for some people in the market, the wellbeing of the others must be undermined. For example, the excessive fiscal and monetary investment has resulted in too high return in the real estate since the financial crisis, so that it could lead to big problems in the other industries as the resource of the whole society has been transferred there.

I think that there are three aspects should be focused on about the supply management policies as the followings: first, the chief task of supply management is to reform the imperfect of the relative price system, to eliminate the excess arbitrage and to correct the distortions of resource. Second, we should change the pattern of economic growth, which should rely on the market rather than the government promoting the private investment through the market-driven and efficiency-based system. Finally, from the view of enterprises, we should change the trend of "the advance of the state-owned enterprises and the retreat of privates enterprises", adjust the unreasonable distribution of enterprises as well as improve the efficiency of enterprises.

**7. Chen Yongjun, Professor and Vice President of China Economic Reform and Development Research Institute, Renmin University of China: New Urbanization is the Key to Reform**

Over the past 10 years, land-centric urbanization pattern, forming the "land finance", has become an important source of local governments to make up the difference. This has directly led to China's urbanization level advancing by leaps and bounds. But it has also caused the biggest problem existing in urbanization, namely there are nearly more than 200 million migrant workers accounting for 52 % of the urbanization level not fully become citizens. How to solve this problem of migrant workers is need to focus on the urbanization construction in the next step in China, and is also the core content of implementation of the "people-oriented" urbanization.

It is noteworthy that, under the fact that the current economy is slowing down and the growth rate of government revenue is declining, local governments still hope to start urbanization by the land and investment, regardless of excess production capacity and the scale of local debt. Therefore, the current urbanization is the dispute between two kinds of "land-centric" and "human-centric" urbanization road, if the urbanization is only generally treated as the greatest power of the expansion of domestic demand and motivation for long-term growth, but it is actually ignored its "people-oriented" core beliefs.

It cannot be achieved to take a new road of urbanization, relying solely on government finance. The fundamental way is to carry out the reform of the land system, the reform of the household registration system and the reform of the fiscal and taxation system. The current financial system and the "land-centric" urbanization pattern are cause-and-effect. Therefore, to solve this problem, we should consider adjusting the financial relationship between the central and local divided by the reform of the tax sharing system since 1994. Only adjusting the financial system firstly, can solve and change the development model of urbanization, from the "land-centric" model to the "people-centric" model.

**8. Professor Zhang Monan, Deputy Researcher of Economic Forecast Department of the State Information Center**

The reform of government expenditures sharing would be the next focus of the financial system reform.

The theme of this meeting is "the adjustment of financial structure and improvement of development efficiency". The report from Xiamen University is to explore how to improve the economic growth dividend in China through releasing the dividend of the economic system, whether the report models the supply management or endogenous fiscal revenue. This is also the theme of my speech today. I think the supply management is not only about the supply of production factors, but also about the supply of financial system. Specially, the restructuring of financial system is the most important in the economic system reforms, and it would play an important role in improving of growth efficiency. We should consider further how to raise the distribution efficiency of capital factor by promoting financial system reform.

The government revenue-sharing reform in 1994 is the turning point of the financial system reform, but this reform is not complete. The completeness are mainly as such followings: Such reform focused on the government revenue sharing between the central government and local governments, but there was not evident reform in the arrangement of government expenditures between governments on different level. As a result, the burden of central finance has been relieved while its revenue has been increasing accordingly. However, the burden of local governments has been added whenever their revenue has been decreasing relatively, leading to a serious mismatch between the finance burden and the finance revenue. The data shows that since the government revenue-sharing reform, the fiscal revenue of local governments in total has decreased to 52 % in 2011 from the counterpart of 78 % in 1993, but its expenditure in total has increased to about 85 % in 2011 compared with 72 % in 1993, the mismatch between revenue and expenditure has been very evident. The further consequence is that the local governments has continued to find new source for finance, and eventually become heavily relying on the "land finance" which indeed leads to many problems such as the real estate bubble and local governments debts and so on. We could find that the share of fund from land transfer payments in local governments fiscal revenue is about 52 % during 2003–2012, specially 72 % in 2011 and 47 % in 2012.

As local governments have no stable tax revenue, they would intervene in the allocation of financial resource. They would collect the funds through the local financing platform or cooperation with the enterprises, specially the local commercial banks. Local governments would be more willing to invest and play a role as a corporation which would lead to a large number of non-performing loans as well as low allocation efficiency of financial resource. According to the allocation efficiency of industry capital, the non-tax revenue would be rather high as local governments have no stable tax revenue, in the end, they would suppress the industry capital obviously, especially the non-tax burden on the industry capital. Or it could be saying that as the government revenue sharing reform is not complete or unbalanced in some aspects, it results the allocation inefficiency of overall economic resources in China, especially of the finance capital and industry capital.

To sum up, the government revenue reform in 1994 focused on the revenue share between the central government and local governments. The next finance system reform should focus on reforms of local governments below the provincial level, particularly about the expenditure allocation. As local governments below the province level actually afford more responsibilities of education, medical, social security and so on, the central government should divide the allocation between revenue and expenditure according to the actual finance burden. The revenue share should be decided according to its expenditure responsibility, and a third party is needed to re-define the allocation of such expenditure responsibility. In addition, we should improve the local tax system in the long term. We should develop more kinds of tax, including real estate tax, property tax, environment tax, or resource tax for local governments, to satisfy their public finance expenditure needs especially the demand for the people's wellbeing. I think this is also the next significant issue.

**9. Professor Wang Luolin, Ad Hoc Consultant of Chinese Academy of Social Sciences**

There is no worry about economic growth in the short term, but it is a formidable task in the long term.

First, there are two issues worth discussing in the report. The first one is that the first sentence of the report, "the excess production capacity caused by the excessive investment in recent three years". However, I think that such production capacity in China was driven by investment in past decades not only in recent 3 years. So this statement should be reconsidered. Second, the last page in the reports says "to appropriately reduce the share of government revenue in GDP through decreasing the non-tax revenue", although such words would be instructive, it could not directly help government operate in practice. Thus, such issue should need further study.

Second, based on the analysis of economy in the future, I am not worried about growth in the short term. My main concerns is growth in the next 5 or 10 years. As there have been unreasonable economic structure and the system problems, it has undermined severely stable economic growth. If we could not deepen the reform, many problems would become more serious.

Such problems could be seen from two events in this year. First, the central government has kept combating corruptions this year. as a result, many luxury hotels and restaurants have suffered declining revenue, even affecting the consumption growth in this year. Such news shows that consumption relying on the public revenue, and corruptions has become an indispensable factor in the sum consumption growth. In another words, the current consumption demand is distorted. Second, the real economy has faced many difficulties since June, and the banks have been the only department without difficulty and whose profits and wages were relative high. However, there is even "money shortage" in the commercial banks, the central bank needs to intervene for liquidity support by setting aside money. This illustrates that the mechanism of our financial sector has been seriously distorted, even it could remain normal only by the "blood transfusion" of the central bank. The two events above illustrate that there are many distortions in our current economic system, and there also exists many difficulties if we want to cure such distortions. If we could appropriately step over such difficulties, a steady growth in the future would be guaranteed.

## Appendix 2: A Survey on China's Macroeconomic Performance in 2013

To keep abreast of the macroeconomic situation and policy trend, an annual questionnaire survey of China's macroeconomic situation and policy was conducted jointly by the Economic Information Daily, Xinhua News Agency and the Center for Macroeconomic Research (CMR), Xiamen University in August 2013. CMR is one of the Key Research Institutes of Humanities and Social Sciences of the Ministry of Education of China. There were 12 questions directly about China's macroeconomic situation and policy trend in the questionnaire, and we invited some domestic economists in relevant areas to answer this survey by email in the early of August, and finally got responses from 43 of them. This survey offered the latest understandings and judgments of experts concerning expectations of China's macroeconomic operation, trends of some major indicators about China's macro-economy, highlights and challenges in China's recent macro-economy and trends of China's macroeconomic policies in 2013. The results of this survey are presented as follows:

1. The General Expectations of China's Macroeconomic Operation in 2013

The results showed that 72 % of the experts considered that China's recent macro-economy operated steadily with a reasonable growth rate. 67 % of them said that China's real economy would grow slowly, 51 % thought that there were systematic risks in China's financial system, 19 % claimed a stable price level, a reduction of inflation expectation and an increase of consumer expectation, and 2 % believed that the income of residents would rise.

As far as the general expectation of China's macroeconomic operation in 2013, most experts considered that China's macro-economy trended to operate steadily with a reasonable growth rate. The important problems which China faces in the macro-economic operating are slow growth of real economy and systematic risks in financial system. A few experts expected a receding inflation and steady price level, and claimed an increasing consumer expectation of residents. Overall, most of the experts were optimistic toward the trend of China's macroeconomic operation in 2013.

2. The Highlight in China's Recent Macro-economy

The survey showed that 49 % of the experts regarded "the general price level keeps stable and the consumption of residents is increasing" as the highlight of China's recent macro-economy. 37 % of them chose "the social security system is developing continually and the coverage of medical insurance is expanding rapidly", 21 % thought the highlight was "new policies and regulations of local governments are introduced, and most ministries have publicly released information regarding the spending on official overseas trips, official vehicles and official hospitality", 14 % said "the State Council has issued a circular Guidelines on Deepening the Reform of Income Distribution System and the income of residents would increase" was the achievement, and 5 % claimed that there was no accomplishment of China's recent macro-economy. With respect to the "New Policies and Measures to Regulate Real Estate Market" introduced by the central government, no experts thought that it would have positive effects on curbing speculations in real estate market and rising housing prices.

To sum up, experts had different judgments about what was the highlight of China's macro-economy. In addition to the opinions mentioned above, nearly 30 %

of the experts made different points mainly including "general price keeps stable and consumption of residents is steady", "the effects of market mechanism become more important in forcing China's macro-economy to transform and update", "China makes new progress in economic restructuring", "the policies on regarding macroeconomic development and control launched by Premier Li Keqiang recently", "China focuses on the coordination between economic reform and macroeconomic policies", "the macroeconomic policy system is built combining short-run targets with medium and long term targets", "streamline administration and decentralization, tax reduction, deregulation and market-oriented reforms of interest rates", "comparing with other industries, service industry expands with a highest speed", "urbanization", "the simplification of administrative examination and approval system", "the economy has not slowed down to the critical level of low growth rate and the economic and financial crisis has not come", etc.

3. The forecast of some major indicators of China's macro-economy in 2013

With respect to the growth rate of China's GDP in 2013, the survey showed that 77 % of the experts thought that it would be "between 7.5 and 7.9 %", 23 % expected that it would be "between 7.1 and 7.4 %", and no one claimed that it would get "7 % or less" or "8 % or more". Obviously, most experts considered that the growth rate would be higher than "7.5 %", a growth targeted set by the central government at the beginning of 2013. Some experts expected the growth rate would be less than 7.5 % and the economic growth in the next half year would slow down continually considering the growth rate of 7.6 % in the past half year.

Concerning the variation of China's CPI in 2013, the survey showed that 63 % of the experts expected it to be "between 2.6 and 3.0 %", 21 % thought that it might be "between 3.1 and 3.5 %", 16 % chose "between 2.1 and 2.5 %", and that no one claimed that it would be "2.0 % or less" or "3.6 % or more". In other words, all experts considered that the variation of CPI would be less than "3.5 %", a target set by the central government at the start of 2013. They claimed that the price level would stay steady and the inflationary pressure would tend to lessened.

Regarding to the growth of China's fixed investments in 2013, the survey showed that 49 % of the experts expected the total fixed investments would increase year on year at the rate "between 20.1 and 21.0 %", 30 % considered that it would increase at the rate "between 21.1 and 22 %", 12 % chose "between 19.1 and 20 %", 7 % thought that the growth rate would be "more than 22 %", and 2 % claimed that it would be "less than 19.1 %". Considering the fact that the total fixed investments grew by 20.1 % year on year in the past half year, it was clear that most experts maintained a relatively steady growth of China's fixed investments.

The investments in real estate had grown significantly in the past half year while China's economy and investment was slowing down. What would the trend of the housing price and sales volume be in the next half year? The survey showed that 64 % of the experts expected a trend of "increasing housing price and increasing sales volume", 20 % considered "increasing housing price and decreasing sales volume", 12 % chose "decreasing housing price and increasing sales volume", 2 % thought that there would be "decreasing housing price and decreasing sales volume", and only 2 % of them maintained a trend of "steady housing price and steady sales volume". In brief, most experts forecast an uptrend in China's real estate market in the next half year, which implied that the "New Policies and Measures to Regulate Real Estate Market" had no positive effects on curbing speculations in real estate market and rising housing prices.

With respect to the growth of China's broad monetary supply (M2) in 2013, the results showed that 58 % of the experts had the expectation that M2 would grow at the rate "between 14.1 and 15 %", 26 % considered "between 13.1 and 14 %", 9 % chose "between 15.1 and 16 %", 5 % thought that it would be "more than 16.0 %", and only 2 % maintained the views that the growth rate would be "less than 13.1 %". We could see that most experts considered that the growth of M2 would be relatively steady and that the monetary policies in the next half year would keep a steady and robust trend which had been mildly restrictive as the past half year.

Will the current policies taken by China's government to carry out the process of urbanization actively and steadily contribute to a higher growth rate of resident consumption in future? The survey showed that 74 % of the experts expected that the urbanization would have a certain positive effect on the higher growth of resident consumption in future, that 12 % considered a significantly positive effect, that 7 % thought there would be no obvious relation between them, that 5 % forecast a certain negative effect of urbanization on the growth of consumption, and that no one thought there would be an obviously negative effect. Besides, 2 % of the experts expected a positive effect on the absolute volume of consumption and a negative effect on the rate of consumption because the process of urbanization required the increase of investments. In short, most experts considered that the urbanization would promote the demand expansion of consumption.

4. The Greatest Challenge in China's Economic Development

What is the greatest challenge for China in economic development? 63 % of the experts answered with debts of local governments, 42 % with the worsening problem of excess production capacity, 37 % with the slowdown of China's economic growth, 30 % with the retaliatory rise of housing price might, which might result in bubble burst of real estate market, and 16 % with the recession of exports. In sum, as far as the greatest challenge in China's economic growth, the survey showed that most experts focused on four factors: the risk of local government debt, the worsening problem of excess production capacity, the slowdown of China's economic growth and the bubble of the real estate market, and these would be the key factors which affect the healthy development of China's economy in future.

In addition, 21 % of the experts made other points about the greatest challenge in China's economic development including "the adjustment of industrial structure makes slow progress and the transformation and upgrading faces the bottleneck problem", "de-capacity and de-leverage", "the consumption demand is insufficient and hard to expand due to such a huge income gap", "faced with a series of dilemmas in the economic development, China has no new effective general strategy design for reform and development, and the recent policy are temporary solutions.", "the deepening of the reform of state-owned enterprises", "the weak foundation of employment", "the strong resource constraint, the rapid ecosystem degradation and social security problems", "removing the unhealthy part of the economy and controlling the risk", etc.

5. The Trends of China's Macroeconomic Policies in the Next Half Year of 2013

Premier Li Keqiang claimed that China had to avoid the sharp fluctuations in economic growth and to maintain a reasonable growth rate at the Symposium on the Economic Situation in July 16th, 2013. The lower bound of the growth rate was the rate which kept the economy growing steadily and the upper bound was the rate which prevented the inflation. Facing the slowdown of China's economic growth, what would China's government do to ensure the economy growing above the lower bound?

As the survey indicated, 86 % of the experts thought that China's government should carry forward the reform of the fiscal and taxation system, proceed with VAT reform thoroughly and unleash the dividend by reforming the fiscal and taxation system; 77 % thought that China's government should carry forward the reform the financial system, revive the real economy and unleash the dividend by reforming the financial system; 77 % claimed that China's government should encourage the initiative of private capital and give market more freedom. Moreover, two experts had different opinions. One said that China's government should maintain the continuity and consistency of current policies and the other one considered that China's government should preset and fine-tune the macroeconomic policies moderately, timely and variously. In addition, 5 % of the experts thought that China's government should launch a fiscal stimulus package and 7 % believed that China's government should restart monetary policies focusing on credit stimulus. It can be concluded that most experts considered that China's government would never launch a fiscal stimulus package with government-led investments and monetary policies emphasizing credit stimulus. On the contrary, it would fine-tune the macroeconomic policies moderately and timely, accelerate and carry forward the reforms of the fiscal and taxation system, the financial system and encourage the initiative of private capital, and further unleash the dividend by reforming systems.

About whether the central bank will adjust the RRR (reserve requirement ratio) or not in the next half year of 2013, the survey indicated that 68 % of the experts considered that the central bank would keep the current RRR steady, 30 % thought that it would reduce the RRR, and only 2 % claimed that it would raise the RRR. Given the previous expectation of M2 growth, most experts considered that China's government should maintain the steady and robust monetary policies and fine-tune them timely and moderately.

Regarding to the trend of fiscal policies in the next half of 2013, the results showed that 63 % of the experts considered that the central government would maintain the steady and robust fiscal policies, that 37 % held that extending fiscal policies would be implemented, and that no one claimed that it would carry forward tightening fiscal policy.

According to the Chinese Pinyin order of their names, the experts who joined this questionnaire survey are:

Chang Xin, Chen Shoudong, Chen Yongjun, Fan Conglai, Gao Bo, Guo Xibao, Huo Deming, Jian Xinhua, Jiang Dianchun, Jin Tao, Lai Desheng, Li Jianwei, Li Jing, Li Shantong, Li Shi, Li Xuesong, Liu Jinquan, Liu Shucheng, Liu Xiahui, Liu Yu, Liu Yunzhong, Liu Zhibiao, Lu Shengrong, Shen Kunrong, Shi Jinchuan, Tang Jijun, Tu Xinquan, Wang Changyun, Wang Yida, Wang Cheng, Wang Ruifang, Wen Chuanhao, Xiao Xingzhi, Yang Zhiyong, Yin Xingmin, Yu Changlin, Yuan Fuhua, Zhang Liqun, Zhang Ping, Zhang Shuguang, Zhang Xiaojing, Zhang Yishan and Zhou Liqun.

Finally, we thank for the active participation of these experts mentioned above sincerely.

The manufacturer's authorised representative in the EU is Springer Nature Customer Service Centre GmbH, Europaplatz 3, 69115 Heidelberg, Germany. If you have any concerns regarding our products, please contact ProductSafety@springernature.com

Printed and bound by CPI Group (UK) Ltd, Croydon, CR0 4YY
27/09/2026
02223591-0001